Cooking Up a Storm

Sam Stern

with Susan Stern, his mom, who got him started

CANDLEWICK PRESS
CAMBRIDGE, MASSACHUSETTS

Contents

I've written this book for kids like me who enjoy cooking or who want to learn to cook. It's full of simple tasty recipes — the kinds of things that my friends and I like to eat.

You'll find a big range of food in here — from snacks you can wolf down while you're watching television to some full-blown dishes you can serve your whole family.

Cooking's a particular challenge in our house. I'm the youngest of five kids. One of my sisters is a vegetarian. Another is an ex-vegetarian who won't eat red meat. My brother's a meat freak. My dad's a bit of a garbage can, but he can't eat chocolate or cheese — his favorite foods. My mom won't eat anything that's tough on her teeth. Me? I eat everything except bananas and broccoli. So catering to everyone means that a wide variety of food has to get served up. It's those everyday foods that I've learned to cook. And that's where the recipes in this book come from.

There's food here for all tastes. There's what I call "big" food — the stuff you want when you've been playing lots of sports, when you're mega-hungry and want some real eating. There's brain food —

treats to get the brain cells and the taste buds awake and the nerves calmed down when you've got exams. And there's food you can eat if you know you're a bit of a couch potato but you don't want to end up looking like a couch. There's food here to keep you fit and to keep you looking fit. And there's party food for when you want to put on some spectacular eating.

Why do I like cooking?

Well, I'm usually pretty impatient, but I can spend hours chopping stuff, blending, whisking, and mixing. I find all that activity really relaxing. The first thing I do when I get into the kitchen is put on some music. I love all the technical stuff that goes with cooking: learning the basics, like how to make pastry, bread, batters, sauces, and soups; doing it the way it says in the recipe; and then, when I'm confident, getting more creative, ignoring how Mom does it, and doing it my own way. You have to take charge when you're cooking, use your own judgment.

I like the fact that when you're cooking, you're using your senses —

It's the feel of pastry, the smell of melting chocolate or fresh bread, the sound of onions sizzling or popcorn exploding. I like it that you're in touch with your food when you do things yourself. You make your own choices. Real cooking is hands on, not just opening the freezer and grabbing a pizza.

Cooking even makes shopping kind of OK. I used to hate food shopping till I started cooking. But now it's a mission to search out the best ingredients. My mom and I often go as a team. There's a real art to it. Did you know that you can tell if a fruit is ready to eat by touching or sniffing it? Or that there are signs to look for to tell you if meat's going to be tender or rip your teeth out? Or that you can tell how fresh a fish is by looking it straight in the eye? I love all that. If there's a rule to shopping, I guess it's that the best sort of cooking comes

from the freshest ingredients. So find a supermarket that suits you, as well as your nearest good specialty shops. And don't eat rubbish. It's the number one rule. Food must deserve to be eaten.

I like to know where my food's from. My old farmer granddad used to say, "You are what you eat." He grew everything he ate and was active and healthy till he was really old. And since I am what I eat, then I think I've got the right to know as much as possible about what I'm eating.

What do I like to eat? Chocolate mousse . . . lemon roast chicken with all the trimmings . . . chocolate roulade . . . spaghetti Bolognese with garlic bread . . . everything that's tapas . . . French onion soup with cheese croutons . . . sweet-potato

fries . . . guacamole . . . chickpea, spinach, and potato curry. . . . The variety of things that you can cook is just amazing.

And it's so easy to do. One minute you can be standing in your kitchen thinking, I'm hungry. What shall I cook? And then a couple of hours later you can have your family or your friends sitting around a table eating a real feast that you've made yourself. Or you're just home from school and there's no one around. So you make yourself some pasta with a tasty tomato sauce. Takes you ten minutes tops from thinking about it to having it hot and steamy and delicious there on a plate. Cooking's never boring. Once you can do it, you'll always do it. It's great to know you can be independent.

A lot of adults these days don't like to cook, don't know how to cook, or don't have the time to cook, which is a bit of a shame, 'cause they're missing out. Maybe they didn't get the chance to learn when they were our age. If this is your parents, you can learn how to cook and then do them a really big favor: teach them.

None of these recipes are tricky. Some are easy; some are really easy. Some are fast; some take a bit of time. (Make some of them ahead.) If there are big eaters in your house, use my quantities. If you're a smaller eater, cut them down. If you've taken a cooking class or you already cook at home, you won't have any trouble getting them down pat. And if you're a first-time cook, then don't worry—just follow the recipes. Good luck, and get cooking!

Brilliant Breakfasts

Getting up can be a real pain (particularly on a school day), but there is compensation: **breakfast!**

This is the meal that gets me up and then sets me up for the day. Even if I don't think I want it, the smell of bacon gets those juices going. Sometimes it's got to be something pretty darn quick: Dad's barking at me to get my teeth brushed. Have I got my books, my sports gear? I'm late again. But I still want something tasty and nutritious. I love **eggs** done any way. A juicy **hot grapefruit** for a cold day. A **yogurt and fruit mix**. Maybe a **smoothie** or some **oatmeal**.

On holidays and weekends, it's a whole different story (and I'm able to sleep in a bit, with any luck), so there's more time to put something special together. **Crêpes**, **silver-dollar pancakes**, a post-sleepover **fry-up**, or maybe some **muffins**. It's a chance to ditch the boxed cereals and get some cool cooking done.

Eggs

Eggs make a great breakfast food—boiled, poached, scrambled, fried. They build muscle, so get cooking them if you're into sports. The protein in eggs is great for your brain.

Boiled Egg

A cracking start to the day.

Directions

1. Fill a small saucepan two-thirds full of water. Add a pinch of salt and bring to a boil. Use a spoon to lower the eggs into the pan.

2. Bring back to a boil. Set the timer for 4 minutes (soft) or 5 minutes (medium). Or 6 minutes if the eggs are straight from the fridge.

Serves 1
Ingredients

1 or 2 eggs at room temperature
Salt

Perfect Poached Egg

You can use an egg poacher for this, but you don't need it. Rely on a steady hand and a bit of science!

Directions

1. Fill a small saucepan or frying pan two-thirds full of water. Add a pinch of salt and bring to a boil.

2. Turn the heat down a smidge. Crack the egg into a cup.

3. Use a spoon to stir the water, creating a whirlpool effect. Gently slip the egg out of the cup into the center of the whirling water (this keeps the egg white together in a neat shape).

4. Simmer gently for 3 to 4 minutes until the white is set.

5. When the egg is done, lift it out carefully with a slotted spoon or spatula. Drain well.

6. Set on buttered toast and add a twist of pepper.

Serves 1
Ingredients

1 egg
Salt
Buttered toast
Pepper

VARIATION
Put dressed salad leaves on a toasted English muffin. Perch a poached egg and a crisp strip of bacon on top for a great brunch.

Scrambled Eggs

Making perfect scrambled eggs is like getting to the next level on a tricky PS2 game. You need a good eye and fast reflexes. Cook the eggs for too long and they end up dry and clumpy. Stop the exact second before they're ready—they'll be softer and sweeter.

Directions

1. Crack the eggs into a bowl. Beat well with a fork. Season with salt and pepper.

2. Melt the butter in a small saucepan on low heat. Tip the beaten eggs into the pan and stir like mad with a wooden spoon for 1 to 2 minutes as they cook, to keep them from sticking to the pan.

3. Take the pan off the heat while the eggs are still soft. Keep stirring for a few seconds. Chuck onto your buttered toast. Eat now.

Serves 1

Ingredients

2 eggs
Salt and pepper
Butter for the pan
Buttered toast

Eat with: Grilled tomatoes, mushrooms, and bacon

VARIATIONS

At STEP 3, toss in any of the following: grated cheese; chopped parsley, chives, or tarragon; finely diced tomato and a pinch of sugar; diced cooked ham; crumbled crisp bacon; diced fried sausage; or diced smoked salmon.

Serves 1

Ingredients

¼ cup rolled oats
1 cup water or milk and
  water mixed
Salt

Eat with: Milk, cream, or yogurt; brown sugar, honey, or maple syrup

VARIATION

At STEP 3, add a few fresh raspberries or blueberries. Or add a dollop of spiced apple puree. Here's how to make it: Chop up a peeled and cored cooking apple or two. Cook in a pan on gentle heat with a little water and a sprinkle of cinnamon and sugar until you have a good smooth puree. Keeps well in the fridge.

Oatmeal

I sometimes eat this before I go off on an all-day trip like paint-balling or fishing. The energy in the oats keeps me going. And it's quick to make — which is good, 'cause that gives me time to get my equipment together. OK, it's kind of gloopy, but when it's mixed with the right stuff, I really like it.

Directions

1. Put the oats and water (or milk and water) in a small saucepan. Heat to boiling, stirring continuously.
2. Reduce heat and simmer, stirring, for 4 minutes more, till thick, smooth, and creamy.
3. Add a pinch of salt and stir. Serve.

Hot Sugared Pink Grapefruit

This one can drag you out from under the covers—even on cold, dark mornings when school looms. Heating fruit makes the juices flow, even when it's been hanging around for a while. So sprinkle your fruit with a bit of sugar and broil it.

Directions
1. Preheat broiler.
2. Cut the grapefruit in half. Using a grapefruit or vegetable knife, loosen the fruit within the segments so you'll be able to spoon the flesh out easily with a teaspoon.
3. Sprinkle the top of each with a little sugar.
4. Balance the grapefruit on the rack in your broiler.
5. Stick under the heat for up to 2 minutes—the top should be sizzling and the fruit warmed right through.

Serves 1
Ingredients
1 pink grapefruit
1 teaspoon sugar (brown or white)

Eat with: Whole-grain toast

WHY NOT?
Try it cold: prepare a grapefruit and an orange as described in STEP 2. Throw into a bowl. Sprinkle with a little sugar and cinnamon (if you like spice). Let it sit for a bit if you've got time. Chop some seedless grapes in half and chuck those in too.

Ingredients

2 bananas, roughly mashed or chopped

6 ounces plain or vanilla yogurt

Raisins, crunchy cereal, chopped walnuts, and/or honey (optional)

VARIATION

⭐ Layer yogurt and bananas with raspberries and crunchy cereal in a tall glass.

⭐ Smush blueberries into the yogurt instead of banana.

⭐ Peel and chop an orange. Layer with honeyed yogurt and crumbled vanilla wafer cookies.

Mashed Banana and Yogurt Bowl

I have to confess, I can't get my head around bananas. I know they're good for you, and everyone else seems to go mad for them. But I'm not there yet. Anyway, this recipe is for all you banana lovers out there — like my sister Poll, who can't get enough of them. When we go to visit my gran, she always gives Poll a mashed banana for breakfast. It's a family tradition. Who knows? Maybe I'll grow into them. This breakfast dish is sooo easy. And there are loads of nutrients in there to power you through your day.

Directions

1. Stir the yogurt and banana together in a bowl.

2. Add any extra bits to suit your fancy.

3. Drizzle honey over the top to taste.

4. Eat immediately.

Ingredients

SOFT BERRY SMOOTHIE
6 ounces of your
   favorite flavor of yogurt
Handful of blueberries
Handful of raspberries
1 teaspoon honey

**STRAWBERRY AND
BANANA SMOOTHIE**
6 ounces yogurt, any
   flavor
Handful of strawberries,
   stems removed
1 banana, chopped
1 teaspoon honey

WHY NOT?
Use any soft-fruit
combos. Don't like
honey? Use some fresh
apple or orange juice
instead.

Two Fruit Smoothies

Running late for school? Not feeling so hot? Fix yourself a smoothie. It's a quick, multi-task food— perfect when you're not in the mood for traditional eating. The fruit-and-yogurt combo gives you the right brain energy to help with concentration as well as nutrients to help out when you're playing sports. I sometimes use a handheld mixer—it's easier to wash. Try out these two fruity numbers, then get creative and invent your own favorites.

Directions
1. Put the ingredients into a blender. Blend till smooth. Alternatively, use a handheld mixer: put the ingredients into a plastic jug or deep bowl and mix everything till smooth.
2. Taste. Add more fruit or honey if you think it needs it.
3. Serve with or without straws.

Makes 8
Ingredients

1 cup flour
Pinch of salt
1 egg
1 cup milk
Butter for the pan

Top with:

SWEET: Maple syrup, freshly squeezed lemon or orange juice, and sugar

SAVORY: Grated cheese and chopped cooked ham

Crêpes

Into a bit of early-morning juggling? Then try crêpes. They're tasty, popular, quick to prepare, and they make easy eating. Team them with whatever extras strike your fancy. If you like, make your mix the night before and store it in the fridge in a measuring jug. Just before you're ready to cook, give the mix a couple of good whisks with a fork. Now it's ready to pour into your pan. Warning: The first one of the batch often sticks and needs to be thrown away. If this happens to you, you're not a failure. Just try again!

Directions

1. Sift the flour and salt into a bowl. Make a deep dent in the flour. Crack the egg and drop it into the dent.
2. Tip a good splash of the milk onto the unbeaten egg. With a wooden spoon, start to beat the egg and milk together in a circular movement without mixing in too much flour at first.
3. Gradually mix in the rest of the flour. Then beat everything furiously, holding on to the bowl with one hand as you do this. Tip the bowl to one side slightly if it helps. The aim is to build up some real wrist action to make sure that the batter becomes smooth while it's still very thick.
4. Add the rest of the milk bit by bit, beating until you have a lovely smooth, thin batter. If it's not entirely smooth, you can always use a whisk to blitz those blobs out.
5. Heat a pancake griddle or small frying pan. You want it hot enough to make the butter sizzle when you toss it in.
6. Use a little pat of butter to coat the pan very lightly. If the butter starts to go brown, it's beginning to burn and will taste bitter, so whip the pan off the heat if this happens.
7. Pour 2 to 3 tablespoons of batter into your pan and immediately swirl it around so that it coats the entire surface.
8. Now cook until you think the underside is done — 2 minutes

or so. Check by flicking up the edge of the crêpe with your spatula. It's done if it's lightly browned and doesn't stick.

9. Tossing time. Or play it safe and use a spatula to turn the crêpe over.

10. Cook the second side till light brown, then serve immediately.

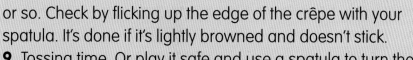

VARIATION
At STEP 6, toss a handful of blueberries into the pan till they're softening and oozing juices. Then pour batter mix over them. Cook. Don't toss— just turn them with a spatula.

Makes 12
Ingredients

2 cups flour
2 teaspoons baking powder
½ teaspoon baking soda
1 tablespoon sugar
¼ teaspoon salt
2 eggs
1 cup milk
4 tablespoons butter, melted

Top with:

SWEET: Honey, syrup, peanut butter, maple syrup, or butter and jam

SAVORY: Cream cheese and smoked salmon or crisp cooked bacon

Silver-Dollar Pancakes

Eat these warm. Pile them high with excellent toppings. This recipe is so good, we had to text it to my brother at college so he could make it for his friends.

Directions

1. Sift the flour, baking powder, baking soda, sugar, and salt into a large bowl. Make a deep dent in the flour mixture. Crack the eggs into the dent and add a little of the milk.

2. With a wooden spoon, beat the eggs and milk, gradually mixing in the flour mixture, as for crêpes (page 16). Mix till all the milk is absorbed into a smooth, thick batter.

3. Use a pastry brush to spread the melted butter onto a large, heavy frying pan. Place the pan over medium heat.

4. Drop a tablespoon of the batter onto the hot pan. Repeat, leaving room between the blobs.

5. Cook for a couple of minutes until the surface breaks into bubbles and the bottoms are just browned.

6. Flip over with a spatula and cook the other sides.

7. Spread pancakes on a tea towel. Cover to keep warm.

Blueberry and Apricot Muffins

Muffins are so versatile: you can throw them together the night before for a quick grab-as-you're-running-out-the-door breakfast or bake them up on the weekends—your family will love you. These also make a great fruity snack for when you're chilling out after school.

Directions

1. Preheat oven to 400°F.

2. Sift the flour and baking powder into a large bowl. Stir in the sugar and grate in the lemon rind. Make a deep dent in the center of the mix.

3. In a separate bowl, beat the egg, then add the milk, vanilla, melted butter, blueberries, and apricots.

4. Tip the fruity mix into the dent in the dry ingredients and stir well.

5. Place 12 muffin wrappers in a muffin tin, and divide the mix equally among them.

6. Bake for 15 to 20 minutes or till done. (Note: Homemade muffins don't rise like commercial ones, but they taste great!)

Makes 12
Ingredients

1 cup flour
2 teaspoons baking powder
¼ cup sugar
Rind of 1 lemon
1 large egg
1 cup milk
4 drops vanilla extract
4 tablespoons butter, melted
⅔ cup blueberries
6 to 8 dried apricots, finely chopped

Ingredients

1 favorite sausage

Olive oil for the pan

1 slice bread, cut in half into 2 triangles

1 big fat tomato, halved

3 or 4 strips bacon

1 flat portobello mushroom or 3 to 5 smaller mushrooms, sliced

1 egg

VARIATION

Try it in a sandwich: Grill the bacon and tomatoes. Lightly fry the mushrooms. Poach an egg. Grill a piece of Italian ciabatta or focaccia bread. Pile the tomato and mushrooms on, then the bacon. Top with the poached egg.

All-Day Breakfast Fry-Up

Otherwise known as Full English Breakfast, because that's how you feel after you've eaten it. I never want this on a school day, but if I'm getting up late after a late night and have time to enjoy what I'm eating, then this is the one I go for. I like a good mix of textures and flavors: crisp-fried bread and bacon, soft juicy tomato. If you're an egg fan, this is for you. Go over the top with some tasty mushrooms.

Directions

1. Preheat oven to 400°F.

2. Stick the sausage on a baking tray and bake for 20 minutes.

3. After ten minutes, heat the frying pan and drizzle in a little oil.

4. Throw in the bread. Cook one side till crisp, then turn over and brown the second side. Drain on paper towels, then put on a plate and keep warm.

5. Add a drop of oil to the pan and fry the tomato halves, cut sides down. Add the bacon and cook until quite crisp on each side. Move the bacon to the plate.

6. Check that your sausage is done; when it is, add it to the plate.

7. Turn the tomatoes. Now add the mushrooms and cook gently, turning once or twice. Remove the tomatoes and mushrooms to the plate.

8. Add a bit more oil to the pan. Crack the egg and let it slip gently out into the pan. Use a spatula to flick oil over the yolk to help it cook. Or if you like your eggs cooked on both sides, then use a spatula to turn the whole thing over. Give side two another half-minute. Serve everything together.

French Omelette

I don't know why people make a fuss about omelettes. They're really easy to make. And once you're down with the basic technique, you can do loads with them. This is a dish that's fast enough to throw together on a busy weekday. But I like to make it when I can take my time to decide what to put in it.

Directions

1. Break the eggs into a bowl. Add the water, a pinch of salt, and a twist of pepper. Use a fork to whisk the eggs with the water and seasonings.

2. Heat a frying pan or omelette pan. The hotter the pan, the better the omelette. Add the oil or butter — it should sizzle.

3. Add the egg mixture immediately and stir a couple of times. Work quickly.

4. Hold the pan in one hand and your fork in the other. Use the fork to pull the edges of the omelette toward the center. Tip the pan so the runny stuff takes its place at the edge. Repeat three or four times.

5. When it's almost set, sprinkle your chosen filling over the top.

6. Stick a spatula under one side and fold one half over the other. Plate. Serve. Eat.

Serves 1
Ingredients

2 eggs
2 teaspoons water
Salt and pepper
2 teaspoons olive oil or
  2 tablespoons butter
Filling of your choice,
  such as grated cheese,
  chopped cooked ham,
  crumbled crisp cooked
  bacon, sliced
  mushrooms, or
  chopped tomato; or for
  something sweet, try
  honey or a little
  warmed jam

VARIATION
Fry diced onion, then bacon and mushrooms or savory favorites. Cook together till soft. Add the eggs and cook through. Serve flat.

Cool, Quick Lunches

Lunch? Don't skip it. It keeps you going. Eat it any time between eleven and three. Often the best lunch happens when you get lots of bits—stuff left over from last night or the weekend—and put them on the table. A bowl of **Chinese-style chicken soup**, maybe, teamed up with a fantastically inventive **sandwich**. Something snacky to eat with **cheese** or some great **fruit**.

Make lunch the top time of your day at school, to power yourself through until you get home. What's in your lunch can cheer you up and rev you up. Take in a thermos of **soup**. Throw a **salad** together. Make school eats as interesting as home ones or you'll end up throwing them away and heading for the fast food.

Serves 1
Ingredients

1 small skinless chicken
  breast
Olive oil
Squeeze of lemon juice
Salt
Chopped fresh herbs of
  your choice, such as
  parsley, tarragon, or
  cilantro
2 strips bacon
1 chunk ciabatta or
  2 slices good white
  bread
1 garlic clove, halved
Mayonnaise
Mango chutney
Tomato slices
Lettuce

Sandwiches

Ban boredom: make great sandwiches.
There are two rules:

1. Be sure that whatever bread you choose (white, brown, whole wheat, rye, focaccia, ciabatta, tortilla wrap) is really fresh.

2. Be inventive with fillings. Sometimes surprising flavors work brilliantly together.

Big Grilled Chicken Sandwich

Have one of these at home or put one in your lunch bag. Use best-quality chicken breast. But even a bland bird gets the star treatment when you grill it and team it up with all these great flavors.

Directions

1. Place the chicken between two pieces of waxed paper or plastic wrap. Bash with a rolling pin to flatten and thin it a bit. Discard paper or plastic wrap. Brush the bird with olive oil.

2. Get the grill or frying pan really hot. Sling the chicken on to sizzle. Cook for 2 minutes, until brown. Turn with a spatula. Cook for another 2 minutes. Poke the bird with a knife to check that it's cooked and looks white all through. Allow extra time if it's a bit pink.

3. Squeeze lemon juice over the

cooked bird and sprinkle with salt and any fresh herbs. Put it to rest on a plate.

4. Get the bacon in there. Sizzle till crisp. Remove.

5. Cut the ciabatta lengthwise. Toast it, cut sides down, on the grill or pan, or in the toaster.

6. Rub the garlic clove on the toasted sides of the bread. Spread with mayo and mango chutney. Stick in the bacon, chicken, tomato, and lettuce.

VARIATIONS

⭐ Slap in pesto, guacamole, or garlic mayo to spread.

⭐ Use avocado and cheese instead of chicken and bacon.

Ingredients

- 6-ounce can tuna, drained
- 2 tablespoons mayonnaise
- Good slug of wasabi or horseradish
- 2 green onions
- 4-inch piece of peeled cucumber
- Squeeze of lime or lemon juice
- Salt and pepper
- 1 wrap
- Lettuce or other green leaves

VARIATIONS
Also great with: canned sweet corn, finely chopped red onion or red pepper, or chopped cilantro.

Fab Tuna Wrap with green onions, cucumber, and wasabi

This best tuna wrap's got crunch, punch, brain boosters, and flavor.

Directions

1. Tip the drained tuna into a bowl and break it up with a fork. Add the mayo and wasabi or horseradish. Taste for strength of flavor. Mix well.

2. To give a variety of crunchy textures, slice one green onion into thin lengths and chop the other into small pieces. Repeat with the cucumber. Add onion and cucumber to the tuna mix. Squeeze in a little lime or lemon juice; you don't want it too wet. Season with salt and pepper.

3. Lay the wrap on a flat surface. Put the lettuce or leaves into the center, then pile the tuna mix on top.

4. Fold, then roll your wrap. Cut it in two.

Zucchini and Cream Cheese Sandwich

Take this to school. Hold back — try not to eat it on the bus. Zucchini is amazing when you grill it. Enjoy the slightly smoky flavor in this wacky sandwich.

Directions

1. Preheat the grill or frying pan to hot.

2. Slice the zucchini lengthwise into thin strips. Brush one side of each strip with a little oil.

3. Lay the zucchini slices oiled sides down on the hot surface. Cook for 2 minutes on each side or until done. Sprinkle with sea salt.

4. Slice the bread in half lengthwise and spread with cream cheese. Layer on zucchini. Add torn herbs if using. Top sandwich or leave open. Delicious.

Serves 1

Ingredients

1 large zucchini
Olive oil
Sea salt
Cream cheese: low-fat, plain, or with garlic and herbs
1 piece French bread or ciabatta
Parsley or cilantro leaves (optional)

VARIATION
Enjoy slatherings of hummus (page 64) instead of cream cheese.

WHY NOT?

Make a great salad with a load of zucchini, cooked as described above. Chop the cooked zucchini and drizzle it with olive oil. Toss with herbs and a bit of chopped chilies if you go for heat, plus lemon or lime juice. Stack on a plate for home eating, or throw into a container for a tasty school lunch.

Serves 1

Ingredients

1 small skinless chicken
  breast, cut into bite-
  size pieces
1 pita pocket

COATING
1 tablespoon lemon juice
1 garlic clove, chopped
Good pinch of cumin
Good pinch of turmeric
Handful of chopped
  cilantro (optional)
Salt

FILLINGS
1 tablespoon plain
  yogurt
1 tablespoon hummus
  (page 64)
Mango chutney
Cucumber, diced
Tomato, diced
Lettuce leaves, torn up

VARIATION
Skip the chicken. Fry cubes of cold cooked potatoes in a little oil with chopped onion, garlic, cilantro, cumin, turmeric, salt, and lemon juice. When cooked, enjoy with the hummus filling and salad.

Spiced Chicken in Pita with Hummus

I really like the mix of cool and spicy flavors in this tasty combo. And it's a great way for eating al fresco (outside) because the pita pocket keeps you from spilling all over your shirt.

Directions

1. Mix the coating ingredients in a bowl. Add the uncooked chicken pieces and toss them.

2. Heat a frying pan. Use tongs to drop the chicken to sizzle in the pan. Turn, and turn again, till cooked through. Poke with a knife to check for doneness (white all through). Remove promptly, or the chicken will overcook and get leathery.

3. Mix the yogurt and hummus together in a small bowl.

4. Warm the pita in a toaster or microwave (don't zap for too long or it will get chewy!).

5. Cut the pita open lengthwise. Slather with mango chutney and hummus mixture. Stuff with lettuce and spicy cooked chicken.

Peanut Butter and Jelly Sandwich

Don't laugh. I like it.

Directions

1. Spread one slice of bread with peanut butter. One with jelly.

2. Slap them together. Eat. Mmmm. . . .

Serves 1

Ingredients

2 slices white bread
Peanut butter
Favorite jam or jelly

Ingredients

3 portobello or 8 smaller
  mushrooms
1 tablespoon butter
Light olive oil
1 or 2 slices bread
Salt and pepper
Good squeeze of lemon
  juice

Mushrooms on Toast

I didn't think much of mushrooms until I discovered this little dish. Mushrooms can have real character. Big in size and dark in taste. My granddad used to search the fields at five in the morning for them, but you can get fresh ones in any good grocery store.

Directions

1. Peel the mushrooms: find a loose edge and, using your fingers, just peel away until the mushroom looks naked. If you're using small mushrooms, wash them and blot them dry on paper towels.

2. Cut off stems, then slice the mushrooms across quite thickly.

3. Heat a frying pan, then add the butter and a glug of light olive oil. The oil tastes good, is better for you than butter, and keeps the butter from burning. Don't use too much: mushrooms soak up grease, so it's better to add more oil if your fungi are looking dry than to use too much to begin with.

4. Use a spatula to turn the mushrooms as they cook so you catch each surface.

5. When they're almost done, stick the bread in the toaster.

6. The mushrooms should be shedding some of their lovely juices by now. So sprinkle on some salt and pepper, and squeeze on the lemon juice.

7. Pile the mushrooms onto hot toast and pour on the juices. Lovely!

Tomato Bruschetta

Just about my favorite. This works with any full-flavored tomato. Variety of bread is key here. Ciabatta picks up all those great flavors. Grill or toast till it's marked for an authentic effect. This makes for a really healthy lunch (or breakfast, or snack. . .). Tomatoes are packed with good things that protect the body from disease, and olive oil is one fat that's actually good for you. Rub a halved garlic clove over the bread if you don't want to add it to your tomatoes.

Serves 1
Ingredients

3 tomatoes, roughly chopped
1 garlic clove, chopped or minced
Plenty of fresh basil, thyme, or oregano
Salt and pepper
Extra-virgin olive oil
2 slices ciabatta or other open-textured bread

Directions
1. Preheat grill or toaster oven.
2. In a bowl, mix the tomatoes, garlic, herbs, some salt and pepper, and a drizzle of oil.
3. Toast or grill sliced bread.
4. Drizzle some oil on the toast.
5. Pile the tomato mix on the toast. Eat immediately.

Soup

QUESTION: What's usually hot but always cool?

ANSWER: Soup.

You can use just about anything to make soup. Sneakers, skateboards . . . No, seriously. Try out ingredients that you think will work. Sweat everything down in a bit of butter or oil. Grab yourself the right stock. Throw in fresh herbs. You'll have a great bowl of lunch in front of you pretty darn quick.

Carrot Soup
with Coconut and Cilantro

This great Thai-style soup is so sweet that you could almost believe it's not healthy, but it's full of great body boosters and improves night vision.

Serves 4
Ingredients

4 tablespoons butter
1 onion, chopped
Pinch of salt
10 carrots, peeled and chopped
2 potatoes, peeled and chopped
Handful of chopped cilantro
4 cups vegetable stock or water; or 3 cups water plus 1 cup chicken stock
½ cup coconut milk
Juice of 1 orange
2 limes, cut into wedges
Salt and pepper

Directions

1. Melt the butter in a heavy-bottomed saucepan. Tip in the onion with a pinch of salt. Cook gently on low heat for about 5 minutes to soften without browning.

2. Add the carrots and potatoes. Stir. Cover and leave to sweat for 10 minutes.

3. Add the cilantro, stock or water, coconut milk, orange juice, a squeeze of lime, and some salt and pepper.

4. Bring to a boil, then reduce heat and simmer, covered, till the carrots are soft. This could take 30 to 40 minutes, depending on the carrots.

5. Let cool, then liquidize in a blender till smooth. Reheat gently, stirring, and check seasoning. Serve with lime wedges for squeezing.

Top Tomato Soup

The best—it's tomatoey and creamy. Roasting tomatoes really brings out their flavor, and roasting garlic makes it soft and sweet.

Directions

1. Preheat oven to 425°F.

2. Set the tomatoes on a large baking tray. Drizzle with a little olive oil. Roast for 20 to 25 minutes till their skins split.

3. While the tomatoes are roasting, put 2 tablespoons of the olive oil in a large saucepan over low heat. Add the onions, carrot, and celery, and sauté them, stirring occasionally with a wooden spoon, for 5 to 10 minutes till soft but not browned.

4. Chop a bit off the top of the garlic head and separate the cloves. Put them on the baking tray with the tomatoes and drizzle with oil. Roast till soft—10 to 15 minutes.

5. Remove the roasted tomatoes and garlic from the oven. Smush the garlic flesh out of its skins. Be careful—it's hot!

6. Tip tomatoes and garlic into the saucepan with the rest of the veggies. Add the water, herbs, sugar, salt, and pepper. Bring to a boil, then cover and simmer for 30 minutes.

7. Remove from the heat and cool for a few minutes, then blitz in a blender till really smooth.

Serves 6
Ingredients

8 to 10 medium tomatoes with the stems removed

3 to 4 tablespoons olive oil

2 large onions, chopped

1 carrot, chopped

1 stick celery, chopped

1 head of garlic

2 cups water

2 tablespoons chopped parsley or cilantro

2 teaspoons sugar

Salt and pepper

Eat with: Croutons; homemade or good bought pesto (page 121); grated Parmesan or Cheddar; a whirl of sour cream; or basil leaves smashed with a bit of balsamic vinegar, salt, and sugar

Ingredients

- 3 tablespoons butter
- 4 to 5 large onions, sliced into thin rings
- 2 garlic cloves, crushed
- 2 teaspoons sugar
- 1 cup white cooking wine or cider
- 6 cups chicken or vegetable stock
- 6 slices baguette
- ½ cup grated Cheddar or Gruyère cheese

VARIATION

At STEP 4, ladle the soup into ovenproof bowls. Top each one with slices of toast till the surface is covered. Cover with grated cheese. Brown in a hot oven or under the broiler till bubbling. SAFETY ALERT: Hot to handle!

French Onion Soup
with cheese croutons

Got a bunch of cold people around? Give them a big bowl of thick onion soup. Everyone loves it. Cook it up before you head outside, then warm it up when you get back in.

Directions

1. Melt the butter in a big heavy-bottomed saucepan. Tip the onions in, then add the garlic and stir to coat. Cover and cook gently for 15 minutes.

2. Add the sugar and continue to cook gently, uncovered, for 40 more minutes, till the onions are soft and caramelized.

3. Add the cooking wine or cider and bring to a low boil. Add the stock and bring to a full boil. Then lower the heat and simmer for 20 minutes.

4. Toast the baguette slices. Top with the grated cheese and bake or broil till cheese is bubbling.

5. Ladle soup into bowls. Float the baguette-cheese islands on top.

Fast Chinese-Style Chicken Soup

I'm addicted to Chinese food. So I like to take a basic chicken stock and give it an oriental twist. Slurp up the broth with a Chinese spoon, and use chopsticks for the great veggies and slippery noodles.

Directions

1. Heat the chicken stock in a large saucepan till simmering. Add the garlic, ginger, and soy sauce. Cover and continue to simmer for at least 30 minutes.

2. Fill a second saucepan two-thirds full of water and bring to a boil. Add noodles. Bring back to a boil, then reduce the heat and simmer for 4 minutes. Drain and rinse the noodles in cold water.

3. When the stock is done, add the rice wine, fish sauce, green onions, and bok choy or spinach. Simmer for 2 minutes, till the greens are wilted.

4. Add the cooked noodles, cilantro, lemon or lime juice, and more soy sauce if you think it needs it.

Serves 1 or 2

Ingredients

2½ cups chicken stock
6 garlic cloves, chopped
2- to 3-inch piece of fresh ginger, chopped
1 tablespoon soy sauce
4 ounces dried egg noodles
1 tablespoon rice wine
1 tablespoon Thai fish sauce
3 green onions, sliced
A few leaves of bok choy or spinach
Handful of chopped cilantro
Good squeeze of lemon or lime juice

VARIATION
Float some slices of char sui pork (page 75) on top of the soup.

Ingredients

2 slices bread
2 tablespoons butter
½ cup grated Cheddar
   cheese
½ teaspoon mustard
Shake of Worcestershire
   sauce or pinch of
   cayenne pepper
Pepper
1 tablespoon milk

WHY NOT?

Cream the cooked cheese mixture with a wooden spoon. Store in fridge for up to a week, ready for grilling on your toast.

Snacks with Cheese

Cheese is the ultimate fast food — my favorite. Perfect with bread and fruit.

Welsh Rarebit

The number-one cheese-on-toast snack, this is toasted, then broiled in a dish. But it only takes a minute. Top it with a big dollop of homemade apple chutney or your favorite relish.

Directions

1. Toast the bread. Then slap it into a shallow ovenproof dish.
2. Melt the butter in a saucepan over low heat, then toss in the cheese. Stir with a wooden spoon till it melts to smooth.
3. Remove from heat. Working quickly, add the mustard, Worcestershire sauce or cayenne, and pepper. Stir. Then add the milk and stir some more.
4. Spread the cheese mixture on the bread.
5. Stick under the broiler. As the cheese melts and browns, it will puddle up around the toasted bread.

Croque-Monsieur

You find this ham 'n' cheese snack on every café menu in Paris. To turn it into a Croque-Madame, fry an egg in a little olive oil, shove it on top of the hot sandwich, and up your protein.

Directions

1. Butter both slices of bread. Spread one with mustard, if using. Layer ham, cheese, then ham again. Top with the other slice of bread, buttered side down. Press together.
2. Slap under the broiler. Flip halfway through toasting, and remove when the cheese starts to melt and ooze out.

Grilled Cheese

Cheesy! Great for a speedy lunch.

Directions

1. Melt the butter in a frying pan over medium heat.
2. Place both bread slices in the pan and toast till lightly browned on one side.
3. Cover each untoasted side of bread with cheese slices, at least ½-inch high. Watch as the cheese melts. When it's soft and bubbling, with slightly browned edges, remove from heat and slap the two pieces together. Yum!

Serves 1
Ingredients
Butter
2 slices bread
Dijon mustard (optional)
2 thin slices deli
  ham
1 or 2 thin slices Cheddar
  or Swiss cheese

Eat with: Fruit; tomato, avocado, and mozzarella salad (page 43); a sharply dressed green salad

Serves 1
Ingredients
Butter for the pan
2 slices bread
4 to 6 slices Cheddar
  cheese

Serves 1
Ingredients

2 or 3 wedges of cheese
1 tart apple, sliced
1 ripe tomato or a few
   cherry tomatoes
1 celery stick
Potato chips
Apple chutney or other
   relish
Small piece of fruitcake
1 or 2 slices bread with
   butter

VARIATION
PLOWMAN'S LIGHT
If you need to break a junk-food habit, make up your combo from: bread, crackers, or oatcakes; crisp salad with a mustard dressing; cottage cheese; celery and/or carrots; and pineapple, apple, pear, grapes, or any fruit that's around.

Plowman's Lunch

The cheese is the main thing for this. It's got to be good. You don't need much, but make sure it's got a real taste. I like to pick out the ones with weird names — like Helluva Good or Laughing Cow.

Directions

Arrange your ingredients on a plate. Enjoy.

Stuffed Baked Potatoes

First bake your potato. Then stuff it. Cook more of these than you need, and refrigerate or freeze the extra. (They're perfect for parties.)

Directions

1. Preheat oven to 400°F.

2. Wash the potatoes well, then prick three or four times with a fork. Stick them in the oven for 1 hour.

3. When they're cool enough to handle, slice each potato in half. Spoon the potato flesh into a bowl. Add butter, salt, and pepper. Mash really well with a fork. Pile back into the skins and place on a baking tray. Bake for another 10 to 15 minutes.

Ingredients

Baking potatoes
Butter
Salt and pepper

Eat with: Any of these toppings:

✪ tuna and mayonnaise with garlic

✪ guacamole and cheese

✪ baked beans mixed with slices of sausage or pork

✪ cottage cheese with fresh fruit, nuts, and raisins

✪ Bolognese sauce (page 54)

✪ ratatouille (page 88)

✪ cole slaw

VARIATION
At STEP 3, add any of the following: grated cheese; a spoonful of pesto (page 121) or some chopped herbs, Dijon mustard, and a squeeze of lemon juice.

WHY NOT?
Bake a sweet potato in the oven for 30 minutes. Slash it open, and eat it plain or with salt and butter.

Ingredients

7 ounces feta cheese, cubed
2 to 3 tablespoons olive oil
2 to 3 sprigs fresh oregano, parsley, or thyme, chopped, plus a few whole sprigs
4 large ripe tomatoes, roughly chopped
1 large cucumber, roughly chopped
½ to 1 red onion or 3 shallots, thinly sliced
10 black olives
Good squeeze of lemon juice

Salads

Can be as simple as a bowl of crisp lettuce with a great homemade dressing. Or something more . . .

Greek Salad

I love this — cubes of salty feta cheese marinated in oil and herbs, piled on a heap of black olives, ripe tomatoes, and cool cucumber. All drizzled with fruity olive oil and a squeeze of lemon. You're either on a Greek island or you're at home watching MTV. Enjoy this with soft warm pita bread.

Directions

1. Put the feta cheese into a small bowl. Stir in half the olive oil and half the chopped herbs to coat.
2. Toss the tomatoes, cucumber, and onion or shallot slices in a serving bowl. Add the olives and remaining chopped herbs.
3. Top with the remaining olive oil, the lemon juice, the feta, and the herb sprigs.

Serves 2

Ingredients

8 ounces penne
3 tablespoons French dressing (page 120)
2 red onions, sliced
1 large cucumber, diced
2 tomatoes, diced
Handful of chopped fresh parsley and basil, or cilantro
Salt and pepper

Pasta Salad

Pasta works brilliantly with lots of different tastes. So experiment. Throw in the things you like best. Let it soak up the salad dressing while it's cooling. That way it downloads maximum flavor.

Directions

1. Bring a large saucepanful of salted water to a boil. Add the pasta. Boil again and stir. Cook for 10 to 15 minutes, or as package instructs.
2. Drain pasta in a colander. Stick it into a bowl. Add

2 tablespoons of the French dressing, mix well, and let cool.

3. Add the green onions, cucumber, tomatoes, and herbs. Salt and pepper to taste and stir well. Add remaining dressing and stir again.

VARIATIONS

Add any of the following to pasta salad:

- ✪ a can of drained tuna
- ✪ cubes of mild cheese
- ✪ chopped hard-boiled egg with bits of cooked bacon

VARIATION
At STEP 2 dunk the bread in pesto before baking.

Serves 4 to 6

Ingredients

1 small crusty loaf of bread, cut into chunks
2 tablespoons olive oil
Sea salt
4 tomatoes, chopped
½ fat cucumber, peeled and cubed
1 red onion, chopped
1 garlic clove, chopped
Handful of chopped fresh basil or parsley
1 tablespoon red wine vinegar
Pinch of sugar
Pepper

Italian Panzanella Salad

The bread's the key to this — don't use a boring sliced loaf. Get ciabatta or a crunchy crusty job. It's great for soaking up all the punchy flavors.

Directions

1. Preheat oven to 400°F.

2. Drizzle half the olive oil on a baking tray and sprinkle with a little sea salt. Tip bread chunks onto the tray and turn them to coat. Bake till golden (5 to 10 minutes).

3. Chuck the veggies, garlic, and herbs into a bowl. Add bread while still warm.

4. Drizzle the remaining oil over the salad. Season vinegar with sugar, salt, and pepper, add, and stir gently to mix. Let stand for 10 minutes before eating.

Tomato, Avocado, and Mozzarella Salad

Buffalo mozzarella is a cheese made from water buffalo milk. Weird! But its creamy taste is perfect for this. Use the best mozzarella you can find, not the stuff sold in blocks. That's only good for topping pizzas.

Directions

1. Slice the avocado in half, cutting around the pit. Twist the halves apart and ease out the pit with a knife. Peel and slice.
2. Alternate overlapping slices of the tomatoes, cheese, and avocado on a plate.
3. Drizzle with dressing.
4. Distribute basil leaves over the top.

Serves 2
Ingredients
French dressing (page 120)
1 large ripe avocado
2 large tomatoes, thinly sliced
8 ounces mozzarella cheese, thinly sliced
Fresh basil leaves

Eat with: A slice of good French or Italian bread

School Recovery

Hey, school's out for the day. And if you're anything like me, you'll want to slump down on the couch for a bit and celebrate the occasion. **INGREDIENTS:** one cat (if she's in), a bit of TV to clear the brain (essential before homework), and something delicious to eat or drink.

DIRECTIONS: Cruise the cookie jar and fridge to see what's there. Hang around the kitchen, putting it together. Avoid all questions, like, "So what did you do at school today?" Treat

yourself to a slice of **banana bread**. Or a **home-baked scone** with raspberry jam. Make a batch of **cookies**. If you've got the energy, a little light cooking is great therapy. **RESULT:** eat, recover, recharge—fantastic.

Makes 16

Ingredients

7 ounces good milk
  chocolate
3½ cups crispy rice
  cereal

Chocolate Crispy Crunchies

A great way to get your chocolate fix.

Directions

1. Partially fill a saucepan or the bottom of a double boiler with water and set to simmer over medium heat. Break the chocolate into a heatproof bowl or the top pan of the double boiler.

2. When water is simmering, place the bowl or pan of chocolate pieces over it, making sure the bottom of the bowl doesn't touch the water. As the chocolate melts, stir with a wooden spoon till smooth.

3. Remove the bowl from the pan and the pan from the heat.

4. Tip the cereal into the melted chocolate. Stir with a metal spoon to coat.

5. Using 2 metal spoons, drop chocolate mixture onto waxed paper. Set on a wire rack to cool. Store crunchies in an airtight container.

Polly's Gingersnaps

Nobody makes these better than my sister. They're very gingery and totally delicious.

Directions

1. Preheat oven to 375°F. Butter a couple of large baking sheets.

2. Sift the flour, baking powder, baking soda, salt, ginger, and cinnamon (if using) into a large mixing bowl.

3. Throw the butter into the bowl and rub it into the mixture with your fingertips till it looks like very fine bread crumbs. Stir in the sugar.

4. Add the corn syrup. Use a fork to stir into a soft dough. If it's too dry, add a little more syrup.

5. Roll the dough into 14 or so small balls and distribute on the sheets, leaving plenty of room between the balls. They spread.

6. Flatten each ball slightly, using the bottom of a mug. Bake for 15 to 20 minutes, till browned (watch that they don't burn).

7. Let them cool on the sheets until they crisp up, then move them to a rack. When cooled completely, store in an airtight container to keep them really crisp and crunchy. Don't store with other cookies—the flavor travels.

Makes 14
Ingredients

1 cup flour
1 teaspoon baking powder
1¼ teaspoons baking soda
¼ teaspoon salt
2 teaspoons ground ginger
Pinch of cinnamon (optional)
4 tablespoons butter, softened, plus extra to grease the baking sheets
¼ cup brown sugar
2 tablespoons corn syrup

VARIATION
Use white sugar instead of brown sugar for softer cookies.

Makes 16

Ingredients

- 14 tablespoons butter, well softened
- ⅓ cup sugar, plus extra for rolling and sprinkling
- 2 cups flour
- 1 teaspoon baking powder
- ¼ teaspoon baking soda
- Pinch of salt
- ½ teaspoon vanilla extract

VARIATION
Make one big shortbread cookie. Just before eating, top with whipped cream, strawberries, and/or raspberries.

Makes 16

Ingredients

- 11 tablespoons butter, softened
- ¾ cup sugar
- 2 cups flour
- 2 teaspoons baking powder
- 1 teaspoon ground cinnamon
- 3 ounces dark or milk chocolate, or ⅓ cup chocolate chips
- 2 tablespoons orange juice

Vanilla Shortbread

I used to take these into school for fund-raisers when I was a kid. We'd sandwich them with jam. Or ice them in bright colors. Sad thing is, I still really like them.

Directions

1. Preheat oven to 300°F. Butter two baking sheets. Line with baking parchment (optional).
2. Cream the softened butter and the sugar with a wooden spoon. Beat until mixture is pale and soft.
3. Sift in the flour, baking powder, baking soda, and salt. Add the vanilla extract. Beat everything together with the spoon, then finish off with your hands, forming the dough into a smooth, soft ball.
4. Place the dough on a smooth surface lightly dusted with flour and sugar. Roll the dough to about ¼-inch thick. Cut out circles or other cool shapes with a cutter. Place on baking sheets.
5. Bake for 30 to 35 minutes. Sprinkle with a little sugar. Leave on the sheets to firm up, then store in an airtight container.

Chocolate Chipperdoodles

Part chocolate chip cookie, part snickerdoodle—all delicious!

Method

1. Preheat oven to 350°F. Butter 2 large baking sheets.
2. Tip the butter and sugar into a large bowl. Stir like mad with a wooden spoon till pale and creamy.
3. Sift the flour, baking powder, and cinnamon directly into the bowl.
4. If you're not using chocolate chips, chop the chocolate into

smallish bits with a sharp knife on a flat wooden board. Add the chocolate and orange juice to the bowl.

5. Use a fork to mix everything into a stiff paste. You may need to pull the paste together with your fingers.

6. Place on a lightly floured surface. Use a floured rolling pin to roll the paste to ½-inch thickness. Cut into circles with a ½-inch-deep cutter. Paste will be bumpy. No problem.

7. Place cookies well apart on the baking sheets to leave room for spreading. Bake for 20 to 25 minutes or until pale gold in color. Remove. Sprinkle with a little sugar. Leave on sheets for 5 minutes, then transfer to a wire rack to crisp and cool. Store in an airtight container.

Ingredients

2 cups flour
2 teaspoons baking
   powder
1 teaspoon baking soda
¼ teaspoon salt
4 tablespoons butter, cut
   into small pieces
2 tablespoons sugar
⅔ cup milk
Beaten egg, to brush

Eat with: Jam and
whipped cream for an
impressive teatime snack.
Make tea—in a pot.

VARIATIONS

SWEET:
At STEP 4, add
chopped dates, grated
orange and lemon
rind, raisins or golden
raisins, and cinnamon

SAVORY:
Leave out sugar. Add a
pinch of dry mustard
at STEP 2. Add
1 tablespoon grated
Parmesan cheese, or
cheese and chopped
green onion, at STEP 3.

Scones

Scones aren't just for grannies—reclaim them! Make yourself a batch, and eat them as they are or with a bit of butter. The secret for perfect scones is to keep everything light. Treat the dough with respect. Don't slap it around like bread dough.

Directions

1. Preheat oven to 425°F. Butter a baking sheet.
2. Sift the flour, baking powder, baking soda, and salt into a large bowl. Add the butter.
3. Rub the flour mixture and butter gently between your fingertips with your hands held high over the bowl so that the mix drops back in. Repeat until there are no large lumps of butter, but don't mix more than necessary. Stir in the sugar.
4. Add the milk and mix lightly with a fork to make a soft but not sticky dough. Use your hands to bring the dough together.
5. Place on a well-floured surface. Handle lightly. Roll it out gently (tease it—no pressure) to 1-inch thickness.
6. Cut out 2-inch circles with a floured cutter. Don't twist. Re-form dough. Repeat.
7. Place the circles on the baking sheet. Brush with the egg. Sprinkle with sugar. Bake for 12 to 15 minutes, or till risen, crunchy-topped, and golden. Cool on a rack.

Banana Bread

Grab a slice of this to eat when you're working on the computer. It doesn't crumble like standard cake. Spread it with a bit of butter or low-fat cream cheese and honey, if that's to your taste. This is a brilliant way to use up overripe bananas.

Directions

1. Preheat oven to 350°F. Butter a loaf pan. Line the bottom with baking parchment if you have it and grease it as well.

2. Mash the bananas till smooth. Lightly beat the egg and add to the bananas. Add the honey.

3. Drop the butter and sugar into another large bowl. Beat furiously till pale and light.

4. Tip the banana mix into the creamed butter mixture. Beat.

5. Sift the flour, baking powder, baking soda, and salt. Tip a third of this into the mix and stir it in. Add a tablespoon of the yogurt. Stir. Add another third of the flour mixture and another tablespoon of yogurt. Mix in the final third and add the last tablespoon of yogurt. Stir.

6. Pour the batter into the loaf pan.

7. Bake for 50 to 60 minutes. Stick a skewer into the center of the bread — when it comes out clean, the bread is done. Remove from pan and cool on rack.

Makes 1 loaf
Ingredients

- 2 large ripe bananas
- 1 egg
- 1 tablespoon honey
- 4 tablespoons butter, softened, plus extra for the pan
- ¼ cup sugar
- 2 cups flour
- 2 teaspoons baking powder
- ½ teaspoon baking soda
- ¼ teaspoon salt
- 3 tablespoons plain yogurt

VARIATIONS
Throw in some chopped dates, walnuts, or chocolate chips.

Evening Chill-Out

Evenings at home can be unpredictable. Who's in? Who's out? Just me, or the family? The vegetarians, or the meat eaters? More homework? Probably. One thing I know is we'll all be tired. And another thing's for certain: we'll be hungry. So what we need is no-fuss eating that's totally tasty but pretty straightforward— any sort of **pasta** (faster and tastier than a frozen pizza), **chicken** (not too heavy if you're going out later), **salmon**, or **some veggie favorites**—

food to make us feel good, to get us sitting down at the table, chatting, eating, chilling, and relaxing.

Ingredients

2 tablespoons butter

2 tablespoons olive oil

1 large onion, finely chopped

3 garlic cloves, crushed

1 large carrot, finely chopped

1 celery stick, finely chopped

1½ pounds best-quality ground beef

Two 14½-ounce cans diced tomatoes

4 tablespoons tomato puree

Good pinch of sugar

Handful of chopped fresh thyme, oregano, or basil

½ teaspoon freshly grated nutmeg (optional)

Salt and pepper

A little water or stock

Squeeze of lemon juice (optional)

1 pound spaghetti

Eat with: Freshly grated Parmesan cheese, garlic bread, and a dressed crunchy green salad.

WHY NOT?

Freeze half of the sauce and make lasagna (page 87).

Spaghetti Bolognese

I haven't cracked how to eat it, but I can cook it. The sauce for this — a ragout — is rich and meaty, with loads of tomato. The Italians let it simmer for 5 hours. This one's OK in 30 minutes, but give it as long as you possibly can. Allow 4 ounces of pasta per person.

Directions

1. Heat the butter and oil in a large saucepan. Add the onion and garlic. Cook gently on medium heat for 5 minutes, till soft and translucent. Add the carrot and celery. Cook for another 5 minutes.

2. Chuck in the beef and brown it up, stirring. Whack up the heat and throw in the tomatoes, tomato puree, sugar, herbs, nutmeg, salt, and pepper. Stir. Add water or stock if too dry.

3. Reduce the heat, partially cover the pan, and simmer the sauce for 30 minutes minimum.

4. Taste and adjust the seasoning, adding the lemon juice if you like.

5. Bring a large panful of salted water to a boil. Hold the spaghetti in the pan, lowering it as it softens. Boil for 12 to 15 minutes or according to the directions on the package. Fork a piece out to check if it's tender. Drain in a colander.

6. Pile into bowls and slap the sauce on top.

Spaghetti alla Carbonara (egg-and-bacon pasta)

Egg-and-bacon fans will love this — the hot pasta cooks the eggs. Pasta releases chilling hormones, so this makes perfect eating when you need to relax.

Directions

1. Bring a large panful of salted water to a boil. Hold the spaghetti in the pan, lowering it as it softens. Boil for 12 to 15 minutes or according to the directions on the package.

2. Meanwhile, heat the oil in a frying pan over low heat. Add the bacon and the garlic and fry till the bacon is crisp. Turn off the heat.

3. Drain the cooked pasta in a colander. Return the hot pasta to the pan. Stir in the bacon and frying oil, and allow it to cool for 30 seconds.

4. Sling in the eggs and a little salt. Stir well to coat pasta. Make sure eggs are cooked through. Add half the Parmesan and stir well. Add pepper to taste.

5. Serve with the extra Parmesan for sprinkling. Delicious.

Serves 4

Ingredients

1 pound spaghetti
1 tablespoon olive oil
6 strips bacon, roughly chopped
1 garlic clove, crushed or minced
4 or 5 large eggs, beaten
¾ cup freshly grated Parmesan cheese
Salt and pepper

Spaghetti Napoli

This is all tomato. The first sauce I ever made. My brothers and sisters eat loads of this at college.

Directions

1. Heat the oil in a saucepan. Add the onion or shallots with a pinch of salt and cook gently for about 5 minutes, till soft. Add the garlic.

2. Tip in the tomatoes, tomato puree, sugar, torn basil, lemon juice, salt, and pepper. Stir.

3. Simmer for at least 10 minutes. Add a little water if it gets dry. Taste and adjust seasoning.

4. Pile on top of the pasta. Serve with grated Parmesan or Cheddar.

Serves 2

Ingredients

1 tablespoon olive oil
1 onion or 2 fat shallots, finely chopped
2 garlic cloves, crushed or minced
14½-ounce can diced tomatoes
2 heaping teaspoons tomato puree
Pinch of sugar
Handful of basil leaves, torn and whole
Good squeeze of lemon juice
Salt and pepper
2 cups freshly cooked spaghetti or penne

Serves 4

Ingredients

- 3 large potatoes
- 1 large sweet potato
- 2 tablespoons sunflower or vegetable oil
- 1 large or 2 medium onions, finely chopped
- 4 garlic cloves, crushed
- Salt
- 2 tablespoons green curry paste
- 15½-ounce can chickpeas
- 2 cups water or vegetable stock
- Juice of 1 lemon
- 1 cup coconut cream
- 1 tablespoon mango chutney
- 1 tablespoon tomato paste
- 7 ounces diced tomatoes
- 2 tablespoons ground almonds (optional)
- 4 tablespoons chopped cilantro
- Big handful of spinach leaves

Eat with:

RAITA: Finely chop a 4-inch length of cucumber. Mix with 1 chopped green onion, 2 crushed garlic cloves, 6 tablespoons plain yogurt, salt, and pepper.

Chickpea, Spinach, and Potato Curry

Calm potatoes and chickpeas get together in a really cool sauce. Grab a big bowl of this after you've been snowboarding or playing football all day. There's enough here to warm you up for a couple of evenings.

Directions

1. Peel both types of potatoes and cut into bite-size chunks.

2. Heat the oil in a large saucepan. Add the onions, garlic, and a pinch of salt, and cook till the onions are transparent.

3. Stir in the curry paste. Cook for 2 minutes. Add the potatoes and chickpeas. Stir till coated. Cook for 1 minute.

4. Add the water or stock, lemon juice, coconut cream, mango chutney, tomato paste, tomatoes, almonds (if using), and two-thirds of the cilantro. Turn up the heat to boil; stir occasionally.

5. Reduce heat. Cover. Simmer very gently for at least 45 minutes. Stir in the spinach and cook for 2 or 3 minutes, till the spinach is wilted.

6. Taste and adjust by adding more curry paste, lemon juice, or tomato paste. Throw the rest of the cilantro on top. Can be served with rice, cucumber raita, nan (Indian bread), poppadom (thin spicy Indian wafer bread), and/or chutney.

Cauliflower Cheese

This is great comfort food. The sauce has to be thick and creamy with punchy seasoning and a really strong-tasting Cheddar. You want it smooth, so measure out the ingredients as exactly as you can.

Directions

1. Preheat oven to 450°F.

2. Strip off the cauliflower's leaves, trim the thick stalks, and break it up into florets.

3. Bring a large saucepan of salted water to a boil. Add the cauliflower. Cover. Boil gently for 8 to 10 minutes. Drain.

4. On low heat, melt the butter gently in a saucepan. With a wooden spoon, gradually stir in the flour, and continue stirring for a few minutes until the mix bubbles. Don't let it brown.

5. Remove from heat. Whisk in the milk very slowly, beating constantly so that the milk and flour mix together smoothly without lumps.

6. Put the pan back onto the heat. Continue to cook, stirring constantly until the sauce thickens.

7. Simmer for 2 to 3 minutes, continuing to stir so it doesn't burn.

8. Add half the grated cheese, as well as the mustard, lemon juice, salt, and pepper. Return to the heat and stir or whisk for 1 minute.

9. Put the cauliflower into a casserole dish. Pour the sauce over it. Top with the remaining grated cheese. Bake for 20 to 30 minutes. Delicious.

Serves 4
Ingredients

1 large cauliflower
4 tablespoons butter
¼ cup flour
2 cups milk
1 cup grated Cheddar cheese
1 teaspoon mustard powder
Juice of ½ lemon
Salt and pepper

Eat with:

BAKED TOMATOES: Cut tomatoes in half, place in an ovenproof dish, and top with pesto. Bake in the oven with the cauliflower for 10 minutes.

VARIATIONS

BROCCOLI CHEESE: Use broccoli instead of cauliflower.

MACARONI AND CHEESE: Boil macaroni in salted water for 12 minutes. Drain. Mix into the sauce and bake for 30 minutes.

Serves 4

Ingredients

4 skinless chicken
  breasts
2 tablespoons pesto
5 ounces soft cheese
  with garlic and herbs
8 strips bacon
Olive oil
1 lemon, cut in wedges
Handful of fresh basil
  leaves
Salt and pepper

Eat with:
ROASTED CHERRY
TOMATOES:
Put some cherry tomatoes
in a roasting pan and
drizzle with olive oil. Add
some garlic, fresh herbs,
and salt. Roast for
10 minutes.

Mixed-Up Chicks

Directions

1. Preheat oven to 375°F. Slice the chicken breasts lengthwise almost all the way through. Open out.

2. Spread the insides of two breasts with pesto, two with garlic-and-herb cheese. Close them up.

3. Wrap a couple of slices of bacon roughly around the outside of each one, and lay them in a baking dish.

4. Drizzle with a bit of olive oil and a squeeze of lemon. Add lemon wedges. Scatter basil over the top. Bake for 30 minutes. Eat hot, warm, or cold. Slice up and share. Eat the lemon flesh. And don't waste those juices—mop them up with some good bread.

Garlic Chicken

Cook this for yourself when everyone's out. Garlic brings lots of flavor into your chicken.

Directions

1. Preheat oven to 375°F. Lightly grease an ovenproof dish.

2. Smush the butter with a wooden spoon. Chop or crush garlic into the butter. Add the herbs, lemon juice, a pinch of salt, and a dash of pepper. Mix well.

3. Slash each breast diagonally three times with a sharp knife. Fill the cuts with the garlic butter. Place in the dish.

4. Bake for 20 minutes, till cooked. The chicken should be white, with no sign of pink. Serve with lemon quarters.

Serves 4
Ingredients

- 8 tablespoons butter at room temperature
- 2 large garlic cloves
- Good handful of chopped fresh herbs — mix what you've got
- Good squeeze of lemon juice
- Salt and pepper
- 4 skinless chicken breasts
- 1 lemon, quartered

Ingredients

¼ cup olive oil
3 onions, thinly sliced
3 large potatoes, peeled
  and thinly sliced
8 eggs
Salt and pepper

Eat with: Salad

Spanish Potato Omelette–Tortilla

I first had this as part of a plate of tapas (snacks) when we were on vacation in Spain. It looks like a cake, but it's actually an onion and potato omelette — might not sound good, but it is. Eat it warm in cakelike slices, or try it cold (it's great picnic food).

Directions

1. Heat all but 2 tablespoons of the oil in a deep, large (10-inch) heavy frying pan. Add the onions and cook for 5 minutes, till they begin to soften.

2. Add the potatoes. Leave to stew together gently for 20 minutes. Stir from time to time so they cook evenly.

3. Crack the eggs into a large bowl. Whisk with a fork. Add a pinch of salt and pepper.

4. Remove the potato and onion mix with a slotted spoon. Put it onto a plate covered with paper towels to soak up excess oil.

5. Pour all the oil out of your pan—be careful, it's hot!

6. Put the potatoes and onions into the egg mix.

7. Put the remaining 2 tablespoons oil into the pan and turn up the heat a little.

8. Put the potatoes and eggs into the pan and lower the heat.

9. Cook till set. Give it a gentle shake every so often so it doesn't stick on the bottom.

10. When it looks nearly set but still a bit soft in the middle, run a knife around the outside. To finish the top, place the whole pan in the broiler for a few minutes.

VARIATION

Slice potato tortilla in half crosswise like a sandwich. Cover bottom with lettuce, tomato slices, and ham. Replace top and cut into wedges.

Salmon in Foil

These shiny little packages look impressive. Wrap up your fish with lots of herbs to create cool juices and infuse the salmon with flavor. Keep it nice and light. Share a big plate of healthy fries made with sweet potatoes.

Directions

1. Preheat oven to 400°F.

2. Cut rectangular bits of tin foil big enough for each portion of fish plus some generous extra.

3. Slap fish on the foil. Crowd each with garlic, shallots, herbs, and a thin slice of lemon. Squeeze on some lime or lemon juice. Add a dash of salt and pepper and a dab of butter, if you like. Pull the foil up and scrunch to close.

4. Cook on a baking sheet for 15 minutes or till just cooked through.

5. Put an unopened package on each plate and serve.

Serves 4
Ingredients

4 portions salmon filet,
about ⅓ pound each

2 garlic cloves, thinly
sliced (optional)

4 shallots, thinly sliced
(optional)

Fresh herb sprigs, such
as dill, parsley, and/or
cilantro

4 thin slices lemon

Squeeze of lime or
lemon juice

Salt and pepper

Butter (optional)

Eat with:
Sweet potato fat fries
(page 81)

Impress Your Crowd

Serve up any of these recipes, especially when the girls come around. These dishes are a bit lighter, a bit posh. But that doesn't mean that guys can't eat them. And you can really enjoy yourself taking time to put them together. A lot of girls I know are vegetarians, so there's not a lot of meat here. Look in the other sections for meaty ideas. Here you've got loads to impress: **herb gnocchi with sage and lemon sauce**; dips like **guacamole**, **hummus**, and **tzatziki** with **pita bread stars**; **salad niçoise**; **gazpacho** (which is the coolest soup going—literally); and a yummy **veggie stir-fry**. Maybe you'll pick up some ideas for Valentine's Day cooking.

Pita Stars with Hummus, Tzatziki, Guacamole, and Tomato Salsa

This looks really cool. And it's great for mixing tastes. Thread a couple of warmed pitas together. Stand them upright on plates to make stars. Spoon your dips around them, and get chatting.

Serves 4
Ingredients

15½-ounce can chickpeas
2 garlic cloves, crushed
Juice of 1 lemon
1 tablespoon tahini
Salt
2 tablespoons olive oil
Paprika (optional)
Chopped cilantro (optional)
Pine nuts (optional)

Serves 4
Ingredients

1 or 2 garlic cloves, crushed
1 cucumber, peeled and finely chopped
12 ounces plain yogurt
Salt and pepper
Paprika (optional)

Hummus

Great served warm or cool.

Directions

1. Rinse and drain the chickpeas. Tip into a food processor. Add the garlic, lemon juice, tahini, and a little salt.
2. Pour the olive oil and 2 tablespoons of water into a small saucepan. Heat but don't boil.
3. Add the heated oil and water to the processor. Blitz till smooth. If the mix is too firm, add more water or lemon juice and blitz again.
4. Drizzle with olive oil and store in a covered bowl to chill, or serve it warm.
5. Sprinkle with paprika, cilantro, and/or a few pine nuts.

Tzatziki

This is cool. . . . Give it a bit of time to chill out.

Directions

Mix the garlic and cucumber into the yogurt. Add salt and pepper to taste. Cover and chill. Sprinkle each serving with paprika.

Serves 4
Ingredients

2 ripe avocados (Hass are good)
1 garlic clove
2 shallots or 1 small onion, quartered
Juice of 1 lemon or lime
Pinch of cayenne pepper
Pinch of salt and pepper
1 tablespoon chopped cilantro (optional)

VARIATION At STEP 3, add chili powder for heat.

Serves 4
Ingredients

1 fresh red or green chili pepper
4 ripe tomatoes, finely chopped
2 shallots or 1 small onion, finely chopped
2 tablespoons chopped cilantro
Good squeeze or two of lime juice
Pinch of sugar
Salt and pepper

Guacamole

The best dip there is. Don't let this hang around too long—avocado discolors when it hits oxygen.

Directions

1. Slice each avocado in half, cutting around the pit. Twist the halves apart and ease out the pit with a knife. Scoop out the avocado flesh using a teaspoon, right down to the skin to get the bright green color.
2. Blitz the garlic and the shallots or onion in a food processor or chop finely.
3. Add the avocado, lime or lemon juice, cayenne pepper, salt, and pepper. Blitz again. (Alternatively, mash the avocado and stir in the shallot or onion and garlic.) Blitz in the cilantro, if using.
4. Tip the guacamole into a bowl, cover, and chill briefly.

Salsa

Directions

1. Slit the chili in half. Cut off the stalk, scrape out the seeds, and finely chop the flesh.
2. Chuck everything together into a serving bowl. Mix it all up.
SAFETY ALERT: When handling the chilies, don't touch your eyes or anywhere sensitive, and wash your hands afterward.

Ingredients

8 to 10 ripe tomatoes
1 red pepper, seeded
 and chopped
4 green onions or
 1 small onion, chopped
1 cucumber, peeled and
 finely diced
3 garlic cloves, peeled
1 teaspoon fresh thyme
 or basil to taste
3 tablespoons olive oil
1 tablespoon red wine
 vinegar
Pinch of sugar
Salt and pepper
1 to 1½ cups water to
 taste

GARNISH
½ red pepper, seeded
 and chopped
2 green onions or ½ mild
 onion, chopped
A few black olives,
 chopped
Croutons
1 hard-boiled egg,
 chopped
½ cucumber, peeled and
 finely diced

WHY NOT?

Put a few ice cubes in
each bowl if it's a hot
day.

Eat with: Slices of bread

Gazpacho

This chilled red soup with lots of bits is great for sharing. There's no cooking involved — just slicing and dicing. It tastes as good as it is for you. Looks dramatic with little effort.

Directions

1. Put the tomatoes in a heatproof bowl. Carefully pour enough boiling water over them to cover. Let stand for 2 minutes. Remove them from the bowl with a slotted spoon.
2. Peel the skins off and cut the tomatoes in half. Scoop out and discard the seeds. Chop the flesh.
3. Put the tomatoes, pepper, onion, cucumber, garlic, herbs, oil, vinegar, sugar, salt, and pepper into a juicer or food processor. Blitz till smooth. Add water.
4. Put the soup into bowls. Chill for 2 hours.
5. Arrange the garnishes on a big plate. Sprinkle over soup.

Serves 2

Ingredients

2 garlic cloves
2-inch piece of fresh
  ginger, peeled
6 green onions
1 cup green beans
1 cup sugar-snap
  peas
1 cup baby corn
1 cup broccoli
2 tablespoons sunflower
  oil
1 tablespoon sesame oil
Pinch of sugar
Salt and pepper
1 teaspoon soy sauce
Juice of 1 lime (optional)
2 tablespoons chopped
  cilantro (optional)
¼ cup cashews (optional)

WHY NOT?

Cut whole oranges into boat-shaped segments, Chinese-restaurant style, for a fast dessert.

Veggie Stir-Fry

This is just one vegetable combo. Learn the technique, then put together your own best ingredients. Use a wok or a big frying pan to stir-fry.

Directions

1. Finely chop the garlic. Grate the ginger. Trim, cut in half, and slice the green onions lengthwise. Cut the beans, peas, and corn into short diagonal lengths. Break the broccoli into small bits.
2. Heat the oils in a wok or large frying pan till hot. Add the onions, garlic, and ginger and stir for 1 minute.
3. Add the other veggies in turn, stirring between each addition.
4. Stir for 5 more minutes. Season with sugar, salt, and pepper. Add the soy sauce and the lime juice, cilantro, and/or cashews if using.

Herb Gnocchi with sage and lemon sauce

Light. Lovely. Herby. Saucy. These work best with baked, floury spuds. Girls (and guys) love gnocchi.

Directions

1. Preheat oven to 425°F. Scrub the spuds and pierce each 3 times with a fork. Bake for 1 hour or till soft.

2. Scoop out potato flesh into a bowl. Mash till smooth. Add the egg yolks, flour, salt, and herbs. Knead briefly into a warm ball of elastic dough. Divide into four logs. Cover with a cloth.

3. Put one log on a board, roll it into a long sausage about as thick as your thumb, and cut it into 1-inch pieces. Press each lightly with a fork to make tiny grooves. Store side by side on a cloth. Repeat with remaining dough.

4. Bring a large pot of lightly salted water to a boil. Reduce to a simmer, and cook gnocchi in batches very gently for 10 minutes. When they swell a bit, remove with a slotted spoon.

5. To make sauce, melt the butter in a small pan, then add the lemon juice, herbs, and salt. Pour over the gnocchi. Or top with tomato sauce (page 55) or Bolognese sauce (page 54). Sprinkle with Parmesan.

Serves 4

Ingredients

1¾ pounds baking or mashing potatoes (russet or Yukon gold are good)
2 egg yolks
1 cup flour
Pinch of salt
1 tablespoon finely chopped parsley or sage
1 tablespoon snipped chives

SAUCE
8 tablespoons butter
Juice of 1 lemon
3 tablespoons chopped fresh sage or other herb of choice
Pinch of sea salt
Freshly grated Parmesan cheese

VARIATIONS

PLAIN GNOCCHI: Omit the herbs.

BUBBLING BAKED GNOCCHI: Mix cooked gnocchi with cooked tomato sauce (page 55). Place in a buttered ovenproof dish. Top with grated cheese. Brown in a very hot oven for 10 minutes or under the broiler.

Ingredients

MARINADE
Juice of ½ lemon
2 or 3 garlic cloves,
   crushed or minced
2 tablespoons olive oil

1 pound fresh tuna steak
French dressing
   (page 120)
6 to 8 small new
   potatoes
Handful of green
   beans
3 thick slices bread,
   cut into cubes
4 strips bacon
3 hard-boiled eggs
1 head romaine lettuce,
   roughly torn
4 tomatoes, roughly
   chopped
1 cucumber, peeled and
   diced
2 shallots, finely
   chopped
½ cup black olives
4 canned anchovy fillets
1 tablespoon capers
   (optional)
Mayonnaise
Salt and pepper

Eat with: Buttered bread
or garlic bread

Salad Niçoise

Tuna, salad, bacon, croutons, and loads of other great tastes in a sharp dressing. Pile everything up on a big white plate and slap it in the center of the table.

Directions

1. Prepare the marinade by whisking together the lemon juice, garlic, and olive oil.

2. Slap the tuna into a shallow dish with marinade. Cover.

3. Mix up the salad dressing.

4. Boil potatoes for 10 to 15 minutes till cooked. Drain. While potatoes are still warm, sprinkle with 1 tablespoon of the salad dressing.

5. Boil the green beans for 4 minutes.

6. Roll the bread cubes in a little oil on a baking sheet. Bake at 350°F for 10 minutes or till croutons are lightly browned.

7. Fry the bacon till crisp. Drain on paper towels, then crumble into pieces.

8. Peel and halve the eggs.

9. Remove the tuna from the marinade and dry it on a paper towel. Slap it onto a really hot grill or broiler. Cook for 1 to 2 minutes, till browned on the outside but a bit pink in the middle. Don't overcook; it'll go leathery.

10. Place potatoes, green beans, bacon, lettuce, tomatoes, cucumber, shallots, and all but a few of the bread cubes (croutons) on a plate or in a bowl. Cover with dressing. Top with the tuna, reserved croutons, black olives, anchovies, eggs (yolk-side up and topped with mayo), and capers, if using. Sprinkle with salt and pepper.

VARIATIONS

CANNED TUNA SALAD: Skip the marinade and substitute two 6-ounce cans of tuna at STEP 10.

CHICKEN SALAD: Use grilled chicken breast instead of tuna. Skip the anchovies, capers, and potatoes. Top with curls of Parmesan cheese.

SALMON SALAD: Use salmon instead of tuna.

AVOCADO AND CHEESE: Skip the anchovies, bacon, tuna, and capers. Add dates, nuts, raisins, avocado, and cheese.

When Friends Stop By

Friends and parents at the same table can be, well, embarrassing. Your dad starts to tell bad jokes; your mom starts to fuss . . . So keep them apart. Or cook some great food as a major distraction.

Try my friend Joe's **Thai green curry** with attitude. Chinese-food fans go for **char sui pork**. Just a couple of friends around? Make a brilliant **steak salad** and potato **rosti**.

If they can't be bothered to drag themselves away from the game, dish up **pasta with meatballs and tomato sauce**. Or a great bowl of **chili** with cheese, sour cream, salsa, and tortillas. Try not to spill on the sofa!

Eating outside? Go for **burgers**—beef or tuna or mushroom—stacked with some great tasty stuff.

Be creative with salads, relishes, and all the extras.

Ingredients

- 2 tablespoons grapeseed or vegetable oil
- 6 skinless chicken breasts, diced
- 4 shallots, finely sliced
- 1 stalk lemongrass, sliced
- 2 garlic cloves, crushed or minced
- 1 teaspoon peanut butter
- Grated rind and juice of of 1 lime
- 2 teaspoons coriander
- 2 teaspoons cumin
- 1½-inch piece of fresh ginger, grated
- 1 small green habanero chili, seeded and thinly sliced
- 1 small red chili or cherry pepper, seeded and thinly sliced
- 2 teaspoons Thai fish sauce
- 1½ cups coconut milk
- Handful of chopped cilantro
- Cashews, chopped, to garnish (optional)

Eat with: Bowls of sticky Thai jasmine rice

My Friend Joe's Thai Green Curry

Joe cooks in his own style. He likes to take a bit of a basic recipe, then chuck in extras to make up for stuff he hasn't got. This is his Thai green curry.

Directions

1. Heat a large wok. Add the oil. Tip in the chicken. Stir-fry till sealed—changes color—and almost cooked. Transfer chicken to a plate.

2. Add more oil if needed. Fry shallots, lemongrass, and garlic till soft.

3. Add peanut butter, lime rind and juice, coriander, cumin, ginger, chili (or pepper), and fish sauce. Cook for 2 minutes.

4. Add the coconut milk and most of the cilantro (save some for serving). Stir. Replace the chicken. Simmer for 30 minutes, stirring occasionally to stop the curry from sticking.

5. Tip into a serving dish. Top with cashews and cilantro.

Char Sui Pork

My friends and I used to go to this all-you-can-eat Chinese place in town. They've just closed down, so maybe we ate too much. Now I cook this instead. Pork's a really great meat for soaking up the sweet Chinese-style flavors.

Directions

1. Mix the marinade ingredients in a dish. Add the pork. Leave to marinate for as long as you've got, turning over once.
2. Preheat oven to 400°F.
3. Lay foil over the base of a roasting pan. Put a wire rack on top. Put your meat on the rack. Roast for 20 minutes, brushing with marinade a couple of times.
4. Let pork relax somewhere warm for 10 minutes. Carve into thin slices.

Serves 4
Ingredients

Two 1-pound pieces of pork tenderloin

MARINADE:
2 tablespoons honey
2 tablespoons soy sauce
2 tablespoons hoisin sauce
1 teaspoon sesame oil
Pinch of Chinese five-spice powder

Eat with: Veggie stir-fry (page 68) and plain or egg-fried rice (page 116). Great with cooked noodles stir-fried with garlic, green onions, and bean sprouts.

VARIATION
CHAR SUI TOFU: Use two 8-ounce packs firm tofu instead of pork. Drain out the water and pat dry with a paper towel. Cut into cubes. Stick in marinade. Drain and save marinade for topping. Fry gently in a little sunflower and sesame oil till browned all over. Top with marinade and slices of fried garlic and cilantro. Enjoy with stir-fry.

VARIATION
MEATLOAF:
Bake the mix in a greased loaf pan at 375°F for 1 to 1¼ hours. Eat hot with tomato sauce (page 55) or cold with baked spuds. Great in sandwiches.

Serves 6

Ingredients

2 thick slices good white bread, crusts removed
2 to 3 tablespoons milk
Olive or sunflower oil
1 onion, finely chopped
2 garlic cloves, crushed
1 pound best-quality ground beef
2-inch piece of fresh ginger, grated
Grated rind of 1 lemon
2 tablespoons chopped fresh herbs, such as thyme, cilantro, or parsley
1 egg
Salt and pepper
Flour to coat
2 recipes Napoli tomato sauce (page 55)
Pasta of choice

Eat with: Fettuccine or other pasta; rice; or couscous. Add loads of Parmesan cheese.

Pasta with Meatballs and Tomato Sauce

Back from a soccer game? Meatballs keep the theme going. Put these together before you go out, then stick them in the sauce when you get back. The beef and ginger idea comes from dim sum Chinese dumplings.

Directions

1. Tear the bread into chunks and place in a large bowl. Add the milk. Leave for 5 minutes, then squeeze the bread dry and chuck out the milk.

2. Heat 1 tablespoon oil in a large frying pan. Cook the onion and garlic gently, till soft. Add to bread in bowl.

3. Add the beef, ginger, lemon rind, herbs, egg, salt, and pepper to the bread mixture. Mix.

4. Shape into walnut-size balls. Roll lightly in flour.

5. Cook the meatballs gently in oil for 10 to 15 minutes, till brown all over, turning now and then.

6. Heat the tomato sauce in a large saucepan. Add meatballs. Reduce heat, cover, and cook gently for 15 minutes.

7. Serve over the cooked pasta of your choice.

Chili con Carne

A classic. Give it a long, slow cook. Go for gourmet —
check out the toppings.

Directions

1. Heat half the oil in a large heavy-bottomed saucepan. Tip in
the steak or ground beef. Turn quickly till brown.

2. Lower heat. Add the rest of the oil, the onion, garlic, chili,
and cilantro. Cook for a few minutes till soft.

3. Add the beans, tomatoes, tomato puree, sugar, stock or
water, and cinnamon stick. Stir. Bring to boil.

4. Reduce heat. Cover. Simmer very gently for 1 hour, stirring
occasionally. Add a splash of water if needed.

5. Add the red pepper and stir. Cover and simmer gently for
40 more minutes.

6. Taste. Season with salt, pepper, and a squeeze of lime.

Serves 4
Ingredients

2 tablespoons sunflower
  oil
1 to 1½ pounds chuck
  steak, chopped small,
  or ground beef
1 large onion, chopped
3 garlic cloves, crushed
1 or 2 fresh green chili
  peppers, seeded and
  chopped
Handful of chopped
  cilantro
15½-ounce can kidney
  beans
14½-ounce can crushed
  tomatoes
2 tablespoons tomato
  puree
2 teaspooons brown
  sugar
½ cup chicken stock or
  water
1 cinnamon stick
1 red pepper, seeded
  and chopped
Salt and pepper
Squeeze of lime juice

Eat with: Tortilla chips or
tacos. Top with diced
avocado, chopped
cilantro, chopped red
onion, a squeeze of lime
juice, grated cheese,
and/or sour cream.

Serves 4
Ingredients

Four 5-ounce sirloin or rump steak filets
1 garlic clove, halved
Olive oil
Pepper
½ cup water or beef stock
Salt and pepper

SALAD
Watercress, arugula, baby spinach, or romaine lettuce
2 shallots, thinly sliced
6 tomatoes, roughly chopped
Honey and mustard dressing (page 120)

VARIATION
Tender tuna makes a great alternative. At STEP 1, brush each tuna steak with olive and sesame oil. At STEP 3, grill or pan-fry for 2 minutes each side. Add soy sauce and lime or lemon juice. Bubble. Turn tuna to coat in the glaze. Sprinkle with sesame seeds. Serve on salad and rosti. Enjoy with Japanese ginger and a slug of wasabi.

Steak Salad and Rosti

Perfect for when just a couple of friends are over. Get one chopping salad, another doing the rosti and dressing. You sit back and watch the steak.
(Figuring out when it's done takes a lot of focus.)

Steak Salad

Directions

1. Take the steaks from the fridge 1 hour before cooking. Rub with garlic and a few drops of oil. Season with pepper—not salt, which toughens the meat.

2. Get your grill or frying pan really hot. Slap the steaks down. Timing depends on the heat of pan and the type and thickness of the steak, but as a guide:

RARE: 1 to 2 minutes per side, red inside.
MEDIUM RARE: 2 to 3 minutes per side, a bit pink.
WELL DONE: 3 to 4 minutes per side, browned through.

3. When the steaks are cooked to your taste, sprinkle them with salt and move them to a plate to relax for 2 to 3 minutes in a warm place. Make up the salad and top with the steak (whole or carved into strips).

4. Add the water or stock to the meat juices left in the pan. Heat till it bubbles up a little. When reduced a bit, drizzle over meat.

Rosti

Great as a supporting act. This looks like a big pancake. Cook it in olive oil. Slice it up like a cake.

Directions

1. Boil unpeeled spuds for 10 minutes. Drain. Cool for at least 5 minutes.

2. Peel spuds. Grate coarsely into a bowl. Add salt, pepper, green onions, and dill. Mix lightly with a fork.

3. Heat a little oil and butter in a pan. Spoon the spud mix in and spread it out to cover the pan like a pancake.

4. Cook gently for 10 minutes. The underside should be crisp and brown.

5. To turn the rosti, hold a large plate over the pan. Turn both pan and plate over together so that the rosti turns out onto the plate. Then slide it off the plate, back into the pan, browned side up, and cook till brown underneath. Use a light pan that's easy to lift and turn.

Serves 4
Ingredients

8 large potatoes
Salt and pepper
4 green onions, thinly sliced (optional)
3 tablespoons chopped fresh dill (optional)
Olive oil plus a pat of butter

WHY NOT?

Make the rosti the main event and pile it with bacon and mushrooms, smoked salmon, or poached or fried eggs.

Brilliant Burgers

These are really worth tasting—not just for filling your face. Use the best beef you can get.

Makes 4
Ingredients

- 1 pound best-quality ground beef
- Salt and pepper
- 3 sprigs fresh thyme, leaves only
- 1 tablespoon finely chopped parsley
- 1 small egg, lightly beaten
- Olive oil
- 1 small onion, finely chopped
- 2 garlic cloves, minced
- 4 soft white buns

Directions

1. Throw the ground beef into a bowl. Season well with salt and pepper. Add the herbs and egg. Mix.
2. Fry the onion and garlic in a little olive oil, till soft.
3. Stir onion and garlic into meat mixture. Mix well. Roll into balls, then flatten to the size and shape you like.
4. For cooking inside: Heat a frying pan and cook 3 minutes. Turn. Cook for another 3 minutes. Repeat till cooked.
For the grill: Cook on a grill that's 6 inches from the coals for 5 minutes each side, till done.
5. Toast buns if desired. Slap the burgers in them.

Tuna Burgers

Thanks to the wonder of the tuna burger, all your burger needs are solved. It's not dripping in fat, it's not dry, and it's not red meat. Tuna's power food. Great if you're into sports. Pair it with ginger and spice. Cook these inside—they're a bit fragile for the grill. This is scrumptious with sweet potato fries and garlic mayo.

Makes 4
Ingredients

- 1 pound fresh tuna
- 1 tablespoon Dijon mustard
- ½ to 1 teaspoon chopped pickled ginger for sushi
- 3 sprigs fresh thyme, leaves only (chopped dill or cilantro are also good)
- ¾ teaspoon fennel seeds, ground (use a spice grinder or a coffee grinder)
- Pinch of salt
- Pinch of cayenne pepper
- Olive oil
- 4 burger buns

Directions

1. Chop the tuna into tiny chunks with a sharp knife till it looks like ground beef. Tip it into a bowl with the mustard, pickled ginger, thyme, fennel, salt, and cayenne. Mix gently.
2. Divide into 4 burger shapes. Chill or use immediately.
3. Put a little oil in a frying pan on medium heat. Cook the burgers for 3 minutes on each side (they'll still be a bit pink inside). Turn with care—they're not robust. Don't panic if a bit drops off. Once they're in the buns, they'll all look perfect.

Mushroom Burgers

Don't make this with anything other than big portobello mushrooms. Bake in the oven or on the grill with herbs and lemon to soup up the taste. Melt cheese over the top if that's what you like. Layer up with your best extras.

Directions

1. Preheat oven to 425°F if cooking inside.
2. Place mushroooms on a baking tray. Drizzle with olive oil, lemon juice, salt, pepper, garlic, and herbs. Leave to marinate for 30 minutes.
3. Bake in the oven for 15 to 20 minutes, flipping over once, or grill for 5 to 6 minutes, till done.

Makes 4
Ingredients

8 big portobello mushrooms
Olive oil
Squeeze of lemon juice
Salt and pepper
3 garlic cloves, crushed or minced
Chopped fresh parsley, cilantro, or thyme
4 burger buns
Toppings of choice

Fat Fries

You don't want to be frying spuds when you've got burgers to cook. Bake these in the oven in a bit of olive oil. Great with chili sauce and cool for parties.

Directions

1. Preheat oven to 475°F.
2. Scrub unpeeled spuds. Dry on paper towels. Chop each one into great big boat shapes.
3. Dry again. Put in a freezer bag with the oil and salt. Shake to coat.
4. Tip fries onto a baking sheet. Bake for 30 to 40 minutes, till crisp and golden.

Serves 4
Ingredients

8 to 10 large potatoes
2 tablespoons olive oil
1 teaspoon sea salt, to taste

VARIATION
Use sweet potatoes instead of regular spuds — peel them and use sunflower oil instead of olive oil. Bake till caramelized.

Weekend Family Meals

Well, you've got to talk to them sometimes, so it might as well be around a table full of food, which puts everyone in a good mood. Sometimes during weekends, our kitchen looks like a disaster area. Everyone's in there: Polly sorting out her veggie thing. Tom and me fixing a roast. Mom fussing—checking if her potatoes are done, again. My sisters Katie and Alice hanging around.

Hopefully at the end of it (if we're all still talking) we're enjoying ourselves, sitting at the kitchen table eating. Stuff like **lemon roast chicken** with great **roast potatoes**, **roast beef** cooked on the bone, **ratatouille**, and meaty **lasagna** or the veggie version. Poor Dad gets to do the dishes and the cleaning up before dessert!

Ingredients

- 1 large chicken (organic free-range is best)
- 3 or 4 slices pancetta or strips of bacon
- 2 lemons, 1 for squeezing and 1 cut into chunks
- Rosemary, sage, and tarragon sprigs
- Olive oil
- Sea salt and pepper
- 8 to 10 potatoes (russet or Yukon gold are best)
- 2 large sweet potatoes, peeled and cut into chunks
- Head of garlic, separated into cloves and peeled

Lemon Roast Chicken and Best Roast Potatoes

Tom's favorite. He'll text us to make it when he's coming home. It tastes great and looks cool. Don't be put off by cooking a whole bird. Dress it up like a Christmas tree. Roast your spuds in a roasting pan. Whip up a gravy from the lemony juices. Make a delicious stock from what you've got left. Even my vegetarian sisters wish they could eat it.

Directions

1. Preheat oven to 375°F.

2. Check the weight of the chicken and calculate the cooking time at 20 minutes per pound, plus an additional 20 minutes. Take out any giblets that may be stashed in the cavity of the bird and toss them out. Place the bird in a large roasting pan.

3. Drape the pancetta or bacon over the breast to cover and moisten the chicken during cooking. Stick a slice of lemon on top and fix herb sprigs in between joints and all over.

4. Drizzle the whole bird with oil and lemon juice. Sprinkle with salt and pepper. Slap it in the oven. Set timer for your calculated cooking time.

5. In the meantime, peel the spuds. Boil for 10 minutes. Drain and cut into chunks. Rough up surfaces with a fork to aid crisping. Fifty minutes before chicken is done, add potatoes, sweet potatoes, lemon chunks, and garlic to roasting pan. Squeeze lemon juice over the chicken and season. Return to oven.

6. When time is up, pierce the bird with a knife to check doneness. Juices must run clear, not pink. Remove from oven and leave to rest in a warm place for 10 to 15 minutes.

7. Turn spuds using metal spatula. Shift up in oven or increase temperature to 450°F.

8. After 10 to 15 minutes, remove spuds and veggies from the pan to make gravy. Carve the chicken. Lucky person gets the wishbone. Eat that garlic.

For the gravy: After scooping off excess fat, pour 2 cups water into the roasting pan. Put the pan on the stovetop. Boil hard for 3 to 4 minutes while stirring and scraping any sticky bits off the bottom of the pan. Taste and season for a thin gravy. Remove. Pour into a pitcher. Skim off any remaining fat before serving.

Eat with:
Cauliflower cheese (page 71) and crisp green beans

VARIATIONS: WINTER

✪ Cauliflower and broccoli florets are good tossed with chopped garlic, cumin, olive oil, and a little salt, then roasted for 30 minutes at 375°F.

✪ Cut carrots into sticks, drizzle with orange juice, dot with butter, and season. Place in foil packages. Bake for 30 minutes at 400°F.

SUMMER
Great with salads, new potatoes, peas, ratatouille, mayo, chutney, and relishes

VARIATION
MAGNIFICENT MOUSSAKA:
Add a pinch of cinnamon to your meat sauce. Fry up thin slices of 2 or 3 eggplants. Layer up meat, eggplants, and sauce in a dish. Finish with eggplant and cheese sauce. Bake as you would lasagna.

Lasagna

Layer this up with a totally tasty meat sauce and cheese sauce. It bakes in the oven with no fuss. Make double if everyone's got friends staying for the weekend. In which case, they'll really owe you.

Directions

1. Preheat oven to 400°F. Grease a large lasagna dish or oblong ovenproof casserole dish at least 2 inches deep.

2. Make the white sauce and stir in the Cheddar cheese, mustard, and lemon juice.

3. Spread one-third of the meat sauce in the dish. Add a single layer of pasta. Drizzle with a little of the cheese sauce. Sprinkle with a bit of Parmesan. Add another third of the meat, another layer of pasta, and a little more cheese sauce. Then the last of the meat and a final layer of pasta. Top with the remaining cheese sauce.

4. Dot the top with butter or sprinkle with mozzarella, Cheddar, or Parmesan cheese. Bake for 40 minutes.

5. Remove from the oven and let the lasagna relax for 10 minutes before serving.

Serves 6 to 8

Ingredients

- 1 recipe Bolognese sauce (page 54)
- 1 recipe basic white sauce (page 121)
- ¾ cup grated Cheddar cheese
- ½ to 1 teaspoon English mustard
- Juice of ½ lemon
- 1 9-ounce box no-cook or oven-ready lasagna noodles
- 4 to 6 tablespoons freshly grated Parmesan cheese
- About 2 tablespoons butter, ½ cup grated mozzarella cheese, or ¼ cup grated Cheddar or Parmesan cheese

VARIATION

VEGGIE LASAGNA: At STEP 1, make ratatouille or grill or sauté up a plate of veggies. At STEP 4, use ratatouille or cooked veggies with homemade tomato sauce (page 55) instead of meat sauce. Bake. Delicious.

Serves 6

Ingredients

4-pound beef rib on the bone or 3-pound boned rib joint
2 tablespoons beef drippings or olive oil
Salt and pepper

Eat hot with: Ratatouille, mashed potatoes, or roast spuds (see page 84)
Eat cold with: Salad and baked spuds. Match with mayo, horseradish, a dill pickle, and argula for a top sandwich.

Cooking Times

15-minute blast followed by:

Beef on Bone
Rare: 12 minutes per pound
Medium: 15 minutes
Well done: 20 minutes

Beef off Bone
Rare: 10 minutes per pound
Medium: 12 minutes
Well done: 15 minutes

Roast Beef

The ultimate Sunday dinner. Use rib on the bone for a tasty sweet meat. Boned joints like sirloin or ribeye are also cool. They make for a faster cook and easier carve. I like my beef pink and tender in the middle with crunchy browned edges.

Directions

1. Whip meat out of the fridge 1 to 2 hours before cooking. Check weight and calculate cooking time (see below).
2. Set the meat, fat and bone side up, in a large roasting pan. Run a sharp knife lengthwise down the fat a few times to score it. Season with salt and pepper. Rub with oil or drippings.
3. Preheat oven to 475°F. Put the beef in the oven for a 15-minute blast at this high heat. It should baste in its own fat, but for a leaner boneless cut, spoon the juices over the meat a few times throughout cooking to keep it moist.
4. Turn oven down to 350°F for the rest of the calculated cooking time. Test by piercing with a skewer or thin sharp knife.
5. Remove beef from oven. Set to rest somewhere warm for at least 20 minutes, but a large joint can wait longer while you crisp up your spuds or cook your veggies. Carve in thin slices with a very sharp knife. This one's a top dish.

Ratatouille Niçoise

Check out the full-on flavor of this cool veggie stew. There's a sweet-sour kick in there, which keeps the sisters happy. It's got enough personality to work on its own, but it's also great as a team player with beef.

Serves 4 to 6

Ingredients

Olive oil
3 eggplants, peeled, seeded, and cut into chunks
1 onion, thinly sliced
2 celery sticks, sliced
3 to 4 large ripe tomatoes, quartered and seeded
2 zucchinis, cut into chunks
2 tablespoons red wine vinegar
1 tablespoon sugar
Salt and pepper to season
1 small lemon wedge
2 teaspoons capers
8 black olives
Fresh thyme sprigs

Directions

1. Heat some olive oil in a large saucepan or wok. Lightly brown the eggplant. Drain on paper towels.

2. Add more oil. Cook the onion and celery till lightly browned. Add the tomatoes, zucchinis, vinegar, sugar, salt, pepper, and lemon. Cook very gently for 15 minutes, stirring to prevent sticking.

3. Increase heat. Return eggplant to the pan. Add the capers, olives, and thyme. Simmer for 10 minutes or till the veggies are tender. Taste: add more sugar, vinegar, or seasoning if you like.

Desserts, Yum!

Desserts? Eat them. They're the best bit. They keep the family quiet. Bring one in and they all shut up—reach for the spoons and get stuck in there. Dessert makes everyday mealtimes feel pretty cool. They can cheer up even the worst kind of day.

Use the dessert course to sharpen your cooking skills. Fling **meringues** together. Smash them up for **Eton mess**. Make tangy **lemon soufflé cream pudding**. Treat yourself to **tutti-frutti crumble**. Slice up a **cheesecake** when you've got loads of people over. Make **chocolate roulade**—have a big slice. Or whip up some **chocolate mousse**, my personal favorite. And never eat ice cream without one of our storming **sauces**.

Serves 4

Ingredients

Small bunch seedless
  grapes — red, green,
  or mixed
1 pint strawberries
½ galia melon (if you
  can find it!) or
  cantaloupe, sliced
1 slice watermelon
1 small pineapple
1 mango
2 kiwis, skinned
1 star fruit
1 apple or pear
Lemon juice

VARIATIONS

THAI LIME FRUIT SALAD:
Like your fruit syrupy?
Boil 1 cup water, ½ cup
sugar, 5 dried lime
leaves, and 1 stick
lemongrass for
5 minutes. Cool. Add
juice of 1 lime. Strain.
Add chopped exotic
fruit. Chill.

FRUIT SALAD:
No skewers? Chuck
the fruit in a bowl.
Drizzle with a little
fresh orange or apple
juice. Chill.

Fruit Kebabs

Put a bowl of whole fruit on the table. What happens? People ignore it. Chop up the same fruit, stick it on skewers, and they get excited. Strange. Use any fruit you like for this. Include a few exotic ones for special occasions. For everyday, just see what's hanging around. Even a pear or an apple can look cool skewered.

Directions

1. Keep the grapes and strawberries whole.
2. Deseed the melons. Cut into chunks.
3. Peel and chunk the pineapple, mango, and kiwi. Slice star fruit stars.
4. Peel, core, and chop the apple or pear. Brush with lemon juice to keep from browning.
5. Thread in any order on 8 wooden skewers.

Tutti-Frutti Crumble

This is nothing like the kind they serve at school.

Directions

1. Preheat oven to 350°F.

2. Peel, core, and slice the apples. Throw them into a saucepan with the butter, orange juice, water, and half the sugar. Cook on low heat for about 5 minutes. Turn the fruit with a wooden spoon as it softens a little.

3. Tip apples into a 1-quart baking dish. Add the other fruit. Sprinkle on the rest of the sugar and mix.

4. For the crumble, tip the flour into a bowl. Cut the butter into smallish bits. Chuck in with flour. Using your fingertips, rub butter into flour till the mix looks crumbly and still a bit lumpy. Throw in the sugar. Mix.

5. Spread the topping lightly over the fruit — don't press.

6. Bake for 30 to 35 minutes, till the fruit is cooked and the crumble is golden.

Serves 4
Ingredients

2 or 3 dessert apples (Cortland or McIntosh work well)
2 teaspoons butter
1 tablespoon orange juice
2 tablespoons water
2 tablespoons sugar
1 banana, sliced
¾ cup raspberries
1 peach, peeled and sliced

CRUMBLE TOPPING
1 cup flour
2 tablespoons butter
½ cup sugar

Eat with: Whipped cream, yogurt, or ice cream

VARIATIONS
Team up other classic combos:
★ Rhubarb (cook for 5 minutes first) and strawberries
★ Plums and apples
✪ Cooking apples (Jonathan, golden delicious, and Granny Smith are good) and blackberries

Ingredients

- 4 large eggs
- 6 ounces good-quality dark chocolate
- 2 tablespoons strong black coffee (use a good teaspoon of instant coffee to make half a mug)
- 1 tablespoon butter, softened
- 2 teaspoons orange juice
- Salt

Chocolate Mousse

People have been known to walk out of our house carrying pots of this chocolate mousse. But not if I get to them first. It's quick and easy to make. Eat it from one big dish, in glasses, teacups, or ramekin dishes. Don't bother about piling fruit or cream on top. It's simply chocolatey. Get your spoon in there.

Directions

1. Separate the eggs: yolks in one large bowl, whites in another.

2. Fill a saucepan, or the bottom pan of a double-boiler, one-third full with water. Bring to a very gentle simmer. Break the chocolate into the top pan of the double-boiler or a heatproof bowl big enough to fit into the saucepan without touching the water.

3. Add the coffee and let the chocolate melt into the coffee slowly — too fast and hot and it will spoil. Stir twice with a wooden spoon to combine.

4. Remove from heat. Working quickly, stir in the egg yolks.

5. Add the butter and orange juice. Beat fast and furious till glossy.

6. Using an electric mixer, whisk the egg whites with a pinch of salt till white and stiff but not dry.

7. With a big metal spoon, fold the whites into the chocolate in figure-eight movements. Don't overwork it; you want to keep the air in. The odd spot of white doesn't matter.

8. Spoon the mousse into dishes or cups. Chill for a couple of hours or longer. Delicious.

Lemon Soufflé Cream Pudding

If you're a lemon fan, you'll go for this. It doesn't look special, but it's got two surprises: a soft spongy top that melts in your mouth and a layer of creamy lemon sauce at the bottom.

Directions

1. Preheat oven to 350°F. Grease a 10-inch pie or soufflé dish.

2. Separate the eggs. Put whites in a large bowl and whisk till they form stiff peaks. Reserve yolks in a small bowl.

3. Use a wooden spoon or handheld electric mixer to cream butter and sugar till creamy and light. Add lemon rind, then juice. It may look odd, but keep beating.

4. Beat the egg yolks, and whisk them in bit by bit. Add the flour. Beat. Pour in the milk. Mix. Fold in the egg whites.

5. Pour into the pie of soufflé dish, and set the dish in a roasting pan. Pour hot water into the pan till it comes halfway up the outside of the dish.

6. Bake for 40 to 50 minutes or till risen and golden brown on top. Eat hot, warm, or cold.

Serves 4

Ingredients

4 lemons
5 medium eggs
8 tablespoons butter, softened
¾ cup sugar
¼ cup flour
½ cup milk

WHY NOT?

Stick lemons into your oven for a couple of minutes before squeezing. You'll get more juice out of them.

Makes 8

Ingredients

4 large eggs — use the whites only

1 cup superfine sugar

2 cups whipped cream

2 cups raspberries

VARIATIONS

PAVLOVA:
At STEP 6, use a spatula to shape all the mixture into one big flat meringue. Bake for 1½ hours. Chill. Pile it high with raspberries and whipped cream.

MERINGUE GLACE:
Sandwich 2 meringue shells together with ice cream. Drizzle with chocolate or butterscotch sauce. Eat with chopped fresh peaches and sliced bananas.

Serves 4 to 6

Ingredients

2 cups strawberries

Good drizzle of orange juice

¼ cup confectioner's sugar

1 cup heavy cream or heavy whipping cream

8 meringues

Meringue Shells
with raspberries and cream

Meringues aren't as tough to make as you'd think. This is the best way of doing it.

Directions

1. Preheat oven to 300°F.

2. Grease a large baking sheet with oil. Line it with nonstick baking paper. Wash your hands—any grease will keep the egg whites from successfully whisking.

3. Separate the eggs. Put the whites into a large bowl or the bowl of the mixer. Save your yolks for making mayo.

4. Whisk the whites till foamy, then add the sugar a tablespoon at a time, whisking in between. Keep going till the mix is glossy and thick.

5. Scoop meringue up with a tablespoon. Use another to help get it onto the baking sheet in a traditional meringue shape. Tease the meringue into a good uneven blob. Repeat, leaving space for the meringues to expand.

6. Reduce oven heat to 275°F. Bake meringues for 1½ hours. Turn the heat off. Leave the meringues to dry out as the oven cools.

7. Peel them off the paper carefully. They'll keep in a container for up to a week. Sandwich together with whipped cream for eating. Chuck on some fresh raspberries.

Eton Mess

This was originally served at Eton College during graduation. It was just made of fruit and cream then and looked a bit of a mess. You can pick up meringues at the store for it — it's pointless making your own and then breaking them to bits!

Directions

1. Roughly chop the strawberries. Chuck into a bowl. Splash with the orange juice to soak. Add powdered sugar. Chill for a bit.

2. Just before eating, whisk the cream till it's soft (not rock hard).

3. Crunch up meringues. Chuck them into the cream. Add the fruit. Stir gently for cool marbly effect.

4. Spoon into glasses, tumblers, or big bowls. Get in there.

VARIATIONS
Use all raspberries, or mix half with raspberries and half with strawberries. Crush a few raspberries and use the rest whole.

Ingredients

14 graham crackers,
 give or take

6 tablespoons butter

3 cups cream cheese

¾ cup sugar

3 eggs

A few drops vanilla
 extract

1 lemon

Strawberries or
 raspberries for topping
 (or Chinese
 gooseberries, as
 pictured)

Our Fave Cheesecake

This baked cheesecake is great if you've got friends over or lots of family around. It's got a smooth texture and a cool base. Pile it up with whatever fruit you fancy.

Directions

1. Preheat oven to 300°F. Use extra butter to grease a round 9-inch springform pan.

2. Stick crackers in a freezer bag and bash with a rolling pin till they're in fine crumbs. Or blitz them in a food processor.

3. Melt the butter in a small saucepan. Add the crumbs. Stir to mix. Tip the crumb mixture into the cake pan, and press evenly to cover the bottom of the pan. Firm up in fridge.

4. Grate the rind of the lemon to make lemon zest, then add it with the cream cheese, sugar, eggs, vanilla extract, and a good squeeze of the lemon juice in a food processor. Blitz briefly till just smooth. (No machine? Beat with a wooden spoon.)

5. Pour the filling into the cake pan. Bake for 35 to 40 minutes. Turn off the oven and leave the cheesecake in there to cool and firm up, then chill it for at least 2 hours in the fridge.

6. Decorate with fruit. Or cover with whipped cream and pile with fruit of choice.

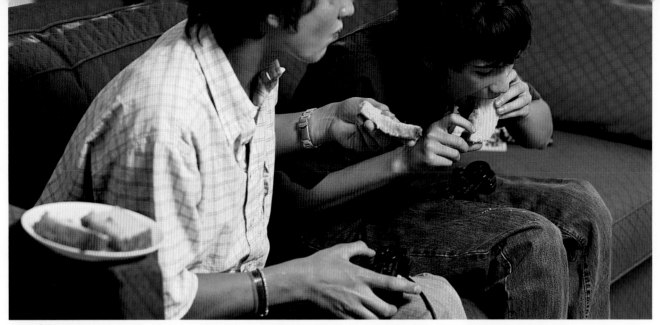

Lemon Drizzle Cake

I can eat half of this in one go. I really love the way the glaze sinks down into the cake, leaving a slightly sugary lemon topping. A great cake for when you're lazing around on the sofa and chilling out.

Directions

1. Preheat oven to 325°F. Grease a loaf pan with a little extra butter. Line the bottom with greased waxed paper.

2. Stir the butter and sugar into a large bowl. Beat with a wooden spoon till creamy, pale, and soft.

3. Beat the eggs lightly. Dribble them into the mix and keep beating. If the mix starts to curdle, beat in a bit of flour and just keep going. It'll still taste great.

4. Sift the flour, baking powder, baking soda, and salt into the mix, and add the lemon rind. Fold this into the mix with a metal spoon, using large figure-eight scooping movements. Gently mix in the milk and lemon juice.

5. Spoon the mix into the loaf pan, spread it, and bake for 55 to 60 minutes without opening the door. Stick a skewer into the cake — when cooked, it will come out clean.

6. Prick the cake top all over. Mix the glaze and pour it over the hot cake while it's still in the pan. Let stand for 15 minutes, then remove the cake from the pan and cool it on a rack.

Serves 4 to 6

Ingredients

12 tablespoons butter, softened
¾ cup sugar
2 eggs
1 cup flour
1½ teaspoons baking powder
⅓ teaspoon baking soda
Pinch of salt
Grated rind of 1 lemon
4 tablespoons milk
1 tablespoon lemon juice

GLAZE
Juice of 1 lemon
2 to 3 tablespoons confectioner's sugar

Ingredients

Sunflower or vegetable
   oil, for greasing
5 eggs
¾ cup sugar
8 ounces dark chocolate
4½ tablespoons water
1 teaspoon instant coffee
   granules
1 to 1½ cups heavy
   cream or heavy
   whipping cream
Confectioner's sugar

Eat with: Fresh berries

WHY NOT?

Make the base the
night before. Fill and
eat the next day.

Chocolate Roulade

A bit of a legend in our house. I can't explain why. Just make it and you'll see. Rolling a roulade and getting it onto a plate in one piece is a bit of a challenge. But even if it cracks up, it doesn't really matter — it'll still taste great. This one's special enough for a birthday party.

Directions

1. Preheat oven to 425°F. Grease a 9 x 13 inch jelly roll pan with oil. Cut a sheet of parchment paper big enough to line the bottom and stand above the rim 1½ inches all around. Fold the paper to fit into the corners and grease very lightly with oil.

2. Separate the eggs using oil-free hands: yolks in one large bowl and whites in another.

3. Tip the sugar in with the yolks. Whisk together till light, pale, and moussy using an electric or hand whisk.

4. Break the chocolate into a heavy-bottomed saucepan. Add water and coffee granules.

5. Put pan on <u>very</u> low heat and stir gently with a wooden spoon till creamy and melted.

6. Fold the melted chocolate into the mousse using a large metal spoon.

7. Whisk the egg whites till frothy and almost stiff. Fold gently into the chocolate mix. The odd spot of white doesn't matter.

8. Pour the mix into the pan. Cook for 12 to 14 minutes, till browned; it may be cracked on top. It will sink when you take it out. Leave to cool.

9. Whisk the cream till just firm. Smooth it over the roulade with a dull knife or the back of a spoon.

10. Lift the short end of the roulade and roll it up away from you so it looks like a Swiss roll. Peel off the paper backing as you roll. It may crack and bits may come away. Don't panic— keep going. When it's nearly there and the paper is just hanging on, lift the whole thing onto a plate.

11. Sprinkle with sifted confectioner's sugar.

Storming Sauces

Here are four great sauces to eat with ice cream. Just pour them over the top or make up a sundae with fresh fruit, whipped cream, and maybe even some sprinkles.

Serves 6
Ingredients

4 ounces dark or semisweet chocolate
1 tablespoon butter
2 tablespoons dark corn syrup
2 tablespoons water
1 teaspoon vanilla extract

Serves 6
Ingredients

2 tablespoons butter
2 tablespoons dark corn syrup
1½ cups brown sugar
4 tablespoons heavy cream or heavy whipping cream

Serves 6
Ingredients

1 cup raspberries
1 to 2 tablespoons sugar

Chocolate
Directions

Partially fill a saucepan or the bottom of a double boiler with water and set it to simmer. Break the chocolate into a heatproof bowl or the top pan of the double boiler. When the water is simmering, place the pan or bowl over it, making sure the bottom of the bowl doesn't touch the water. Add the butter, syrup, and water. Stir till smooth. Remove from heat and add the vanilla.

Butterscotch
Directions

Melt the butter, corn syrup, and sugar together in a small pan. Bring to a boil. Stir in the cream, then reheat gently. Delicious hot or cold.

Raspberry
Directions

Gently heat the raspberries and sugar in a small saucepan till they soften and release their juices. Strain over a bowl if you want to remove the seeds.

Milky Way
Directions

Break up the Milky Way bar in a small saucepan. Tip in the milk and heat gently. Mix with a wooden spoon till smooth but with bits of caramel.

Serves 2
Ingredients
1 Milky Way candy bar
3 tablespoons milk

Party, Party, Party

Shindigs? I love them. Birthdays, sleepovers, a dance, a movie marathon, school's out, year's over, friends around, music's playing—whatever. Eating: chips are OK—but hey, it's a party. So make up industrial amounts of small food. **Quarter burgers**. Slices of your own **pizza**. **Baked nachos** with salsa, guacamole, and Cheddar. Crisp thin **crostini** with cool toppings. Baked **sticky chicken**. Plates piled with **Greek salad skewers**. Slap out some **sausages** hot-dog style with honey and mustard. **Popcorn**.

Prep stuff ahead so you can get out there and chill. Got people staying over? Check that there's stuff in the fridge for a brilliant breakfast

Makes 16 quarters
Ingredients
1 recipe brilliant
  burgers (page 80)
4 burger buns

EXTRAS
Ketchup
Mayo
Pickle slices
Mustard
Lettuce (optional)

Makes 4 pizzas
Ingredients
3 cups flour
1 teaspoon salt
1 packet (.25 ounce)
  active dry yeast or
  2 tablespoons/1 ounce
  fresh yeast
1 cup warm water
2 tablespoons olive oil

Quarter Burgers

These'll keep you dancing. Quarter versions of the rea
thing impaled on toothpicks.

Directions

1. Mix up burgers. Flatten into patty shapes and chill till needed
2. Cook as usual. Lightly toast buns. Stack with a few extras.
3. Divide each burger into four. Secure with cocktail sticks.

Party Pizza Slices

Make up loads of pizza crusts. Freeze. Top with your
best combos. Wear coolest clothes for serving.

Directions

1. Sift the flour and salt into a warm bowl.
2. If using fresh yeast, mix with a little of the warm water.
3. Tip either the fresh yeast mix or active dry yeast, olive oil, an
remaining water into flour. Mix to a dough. Knead on a floured
board for 8 minutes till smooth and springy. Place in a large
covered bowl.
4. Leave to rise in a warm place for 1 hour or till doubled in size
Lightly oil four baking sheets.
5. Knead briefly. Cut dough into four. Roll
into circles or rectangles to fit baking
sheets.
6. Leave covered on baking sheets to rise
again for 15 to 20 minutes. Preheat oven
to 450°F.
7. Cover with chosen toppings and bake
for 15 to 20 minutes. Or do the crusts
ahead. Freeze uncovered on trays. When
hard, store in freezer bags till party time.
Top and cook straight from the freezer.

Popcorn

Yesss . . . party-popping popcorn. It's great and it's low-fat and low-cal. It takes 2 minutes to make from scratch. Get creative with savory bits and spices or go for pure sweetness.

Directions

1. Use a large saucepan with a tight-fitting lid. Pour in just enough oil to cover the base. Heat.

2. Tip in enough corn to cover the base. Slap lid on tight. Hold the lid down and shake pan gently. As the corn pops, it will expand and try to lift the lid, but don't let go.

3. Tip popped corn into a bowl. Eat as is or add a little powdered sugar or a very little salt. Mix and dig in.

VARIATIONS

PESTO POPCORN:
At STEP 3, put the popcorn somewhere warm. Melt a little butter in a pan with a sprinkling of dried oregano or basil. Add a sprinkling of freshly grated Parmesan. Tip into corn. Mix.

CHILI POPCORN:
Melt a little butter in a pan. Add a pinch of cayenne pepper. Stir in one finely chopped green onion. Tip into corn. Mix.

Ingredients

¼ cup sunflower oil
½ cup popping corn
½ teaspoon confectioner's sugar or salt

Ingredients

2 tablespoons honey

2 tablespoons ketchup

1 tablespoon English mustard

8 best-quality pork or pork-and-apple sausages

8 hot-dog rolls

Eat with: Lightly fried onions

Sausages Hot-Dog Style

New York–style hot dogs made with sausages in a honey and mustard coating. Serve in rolls. Great grab-it-and-go food if you're partying all over.

Directions

1. Melt honey in a small saucepan over low heat. Pour into a baking dish with ketchup and mustard. Add the sausages in dish to marinate. Turn to coat. Cover and chill for several hours or overnight.

2. Preheat oven to 400°F.

3. Line a roasting pan with foil. Put sausages on a rack in the pan.

3. Cook for 20 to 25 minutes or till done. Turn and baste a few times if necessary. Serve in hot-dog rolls.

VARIATION
DOGS ON STICKS: Chop the sausages into four. Thread onto skewers with cherry tomatoes and baby pickles.

Sticky Chicken

Sticky wings or drumsticks? Both would work — do one recipe of each with double the dose of marinade.

Directions

1. Heat the honey, pineapple juice, vinegar, and soy sauce gently in a small sucepan. Add the garlic, ginger, green onions, sesame seeds, and sesame oil. Stir well. Remove. Cool.
2. Slap the chicken in a dish or freezer bag. Add honey mix. Turn or shake to coat. Leave in fridge for at least 2 hours or overnight.
3. Preheat oven to 400°F. Put chicken in a roasting pan and squeeze lemon or lime juice over it. Cook for 35 to 40 minutes, turning two or three times. Great hot, warm, or cold.

Serves 12
Ingredients

3 tablespoons honey
¼ cup pineapple juice
1 tablespoon white or red wine vinegar
¼ cup soy sauce
2 garlic cloves, crushed or minced
2-inch piece of fresh ginger, grated
3 green onions, finely chopped
2 teaspoons sesame seeds
4 teaspoons sesame oil
2 pounds chicken wings or drumsticks
Juice of 1 lemon or lime

Party Baked Nachos

Something with a bit of bite. Get around the table with people you like. . . .
Directions

1. Preheat oven to 350°F.
2. Lay chips on baking trays. Top with salsa and grated Cheddar. Bake for 5 to 10 minutes. Done when the cheese bubbles.
3. Serve with sour cream, guacamole, and lime for squeezing.

Serves 12
Ingredients

3 big bags of tortilla chips
Double recipe salsa (page 66)
1 cup grated Cheddar cheese
1 cup sour cream
Double recipe guacamole (page 66)
3 limes, cut into wedges

Serves 10

Ingredients

14 ounces feta cheese
4 tablespoons olive oil
1 tablespoon lemon juice
1 teaspoon oregano
1 large cucumber
20 cherry tomatoes
20 seedless grapes
10 pitted black olives

Greek Salad Skewers

Go global with cheese on sticks. Use toothpicks or wooden skewers to thread up your cheese with great extras. Pop your balloons with them after. . . .

Directions

1. Cube up the cheese. Marinate in the oil, lemon juice, and oregano. Toss and leave for 30 minutes.
2. Peel and cube cucumber. Thread all the ingredients onto skewers—or toothpicks if the cheese is crumbly.

VARIATION

ENGLISH
COCKTAIL STICKS:
Make with Cheddar, pineapple chunks, grapes, and celery.

ITALIAN SKEWERS:
Use mini balls of mozzarella, cherry tomatoes, basil leaves, and olives.

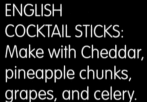

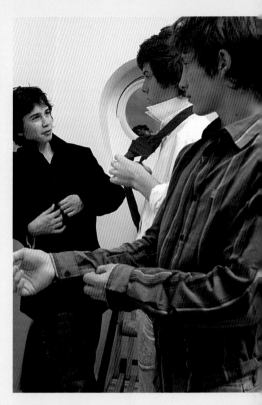

Crostini

Someone you want to impress? Offer a plate of these crisp Italian toasts with impressive toppings. Crunchy.

Directions

1. Preheat oven to 425°F.
2. Cut the bread into thin slices and lightly brush each side with olive oil. Rub one side with garlic and sprinkle with a little sea salt.
3. Bake for 5 to 10 minutes on a tray, checking them so they don't burn.
4. Cool. Pile with toppings just before serving.

Crudités

Crunch alone or dip in hummus, mayo, or guacamole.

Directions

Wash, prepare, and cut vegetables into sticks. Arrange on a plate.

Makes 20

Ingredients

1 baguette
Olive oil
Garlic clove, halved
Sea salt

TOPPINGS:
Hummus (page 64)
Goat cheese and pesto
Caramelized onions
Mozzarella and tomato

Ingredients

Carrots
Celery
Red pepper
Cucumber
Radishes

Exam Survival

WHEN I WAS LITTLE, my sisters and brothers tried to spook me about exams. They said I'd hate them. Guess what? They were right. Now it's me staggering about with a blank look, wishing I was our cat—or anything but stuck in my bedroom all day studying. But I did pick up some tactics from them about how to survive. Like start preparing early. Make a study guide. Ditch the Motorhead—play Mozart. Turn off the cell phone. Don't call your friends to compare notes—they'll just freak you out. Take breaks every 40 minutes. Go for a run. Do practical stuff like the breathing or relaxation exercises my mom

teaches actors. And sort out your eating.

Thing is, everything you eat and drink goes straight to your brain, which affects what you remember, how creative you are, the speed at which you think, how you feel, and how chill you are. So think tactics: Eat the right stuff during exams. Figure out what you need for morning, afternoon, or oral exams. Make sure you can get it all down on your paper without falling off your chair.

My Top Ten Exam Survival Tips should help you manage your panics and maximize your chances. **Good luck.** (I need it!)

Exam Tip ONE

Drink LOTS of water through the day

DO IT. Water keeps you cool and gets you thinking fast. Which is crucial when you're studying and under pressure. Try to drink at least 8 glasses of water a day or you could be a top candidate for dehydration. Dehydration slows your thought processes down and makes you feel like rubbish; learning's a bit harder; your moods swing all over the place; it's tricky to concentrate for long; you may get headaches; you feel wiped out. So not good. Research shows that topping up water levels over a period of just two weeks makes for better results and focus.

Pay attention to the stuff that dehydrates you. Eating lots of salty, prepackaged foods does it. Chips. Caffeinated drinks. Stress makes you sweat a ton. Fill up on H_2O after you've exercised. Drink water through the school day (take a bottle in your bag) and when you're studying at home. Ask to take it into exams. If they say no, see if you can take in grapes instead for energy and water.

Exam Tip TWO

Cut down on caffeine

Caffeine's great for the occasional emergency late-night study session. But not all the time. Caffeine overdose (too much coffee, tea, cola, or energy drinks) messes with your brain. You can't focus. It whacks up your heart rate, keeps you from sleeping, and makes you feel doubly nervous and shaky before you've even started your exams. How weird's that? So keep it low. Ideally, no more than two cups of coffee or soda a day, and after 6:00 p.m. drink decaf.

Exam Tip THREE

Eat breakfast

Eat the right things first thing. You'll work better. You'll get better results for the time you put in. It doesn't have to be a full-out breakfast to do the trick. Flip through the Brilliant Breakfasts section for ideas. It just needs to be right — not heavy.

Exam Tip FOUR   Keep up the vitamins

Treat yourself to some healthy juices, smoothies, and stress-busting tea. When you get stressed, you're more likely to get ill. So foods with immune-boosting vitamins will help get you through. Here are a few ideas for drinks that build resistance to colds and help chill out your nervous system. They're easy and quick to make. Go for one or two a day. If you're not a regular juicer, dilute the stuff with a bit of water.

Fresh Orange Juice
Ingredients:
4 oranges
Water
Ice
Directions:
1. Slice oranges across in half. Squeeze on a citrus press.
2. Dilute with water. Add ice if using. Good to drink through a straw — keeps the acid from getting to your teeth.

VARIATIONS:
TWO-FRUIT JUICE: At STEP 1, replace 2 oranges with 1 pink grapefruit.
ORANGE SLUSHY: Perfect to chill you out for exams in hot weather. Crush lots of ice cubes in a blender. Tip into the juice.

Apricot and Apple Juice
Apricots help you concentrate and they're packed with iron, which boosts brain function. Astronauts eat apricots to speed up their thinking. Puts exams into perspective.
Ingredients:
2 ripe apricots, halved with pits removed
1 ripe peach, halved with pit removed
2 apples, juiced in a juicer, or two cups apple juice
Directions:
1. In a juicer or blender, blend apricots and peach with the apple juice. Dilute with water.

VARIATION:
APRICOT AND APPLE SMOOTHIE: Add plain yogurt to taste instead of water.

De-stress Ginger Lemon Tea

Drink this if you're mega-stressed. Lemon's got cold-busting vitamin C. It motivates the iron in your bloodstream to help you think better. Which — if you think about it — has to be a good thing. But ginger's the part that helps when you're so nervous, you feel sick.

Ingredients:
2-inch piece of fresh ginger, peeled and chopped
Juice of 1 lemon
Honey to taste or pinch of sugar
Hot water

Directions:
1. Put the ginger in a mug. Pour in boiling water from the kettle. Let it sit for a couple of minutes to infuse.
2. Squeeze in the lemon juice, then add the honey or sugar to taste. Stir. Sip slowly.

Banana, Blueberry, and Raspberry Ice Cream Smoothie

Try this when you're feeling too uptight to eat or you deserve a treat. Bananas keep you going and are one of the best stress busters around. The blueberries and raspberries feed your brain. The ice cream gives you an excuse to eat ice cream!

Ingredients:
Handful of raspberries
Handful of blueberries
I banana
2 scoops vanilla ice cream
½ cup milk

Directions:
Blitz all the ingredients in a blender or with a handheld mixer.

VARIATION: On exam day, if you can't face solid food, skip the ice cream, increase the milk to 1 cup, and add 1 teaspoon of honey.

Carrot, Apple, and Ginger Juice

Carrot and apple make this one of the healthiest combos going. The ginger gives it a nausea-fighting edge that kicks in as soon as you drink it.

Ingredients:
4 carrots, washed
3 apples, washed and cored
1-inch piece of fresh ginger, peeled

Directions:
1. Cut the apples so they'll fit through the feeder tube of your juicer or into a food processor. Place a jug under the juicer's spout, if using.
2. Push the carrots, apples, and then the ginger through the juicer or into the food processor.
3. Drink immediately.

VARIATION: If you don't have fresh ginger, at STEP 2, stir in a pinch or two of ground ginger.

Eat feel-good foods

Ever heard of tryptophan? No? It's in chicken, turkey, fish, cheese, eggs, milk, beans, peas, soy, nuts, avocados, and pineapples. It's part of a protein that triggers the serotonin in your brain, which chills you out and helps you to focus.

. . . and brain boosters

Like any food containing iron: egg yolks, baked beans, lentils, green vegetables, apricots, turkey, and beef. If you're low on iron (like half of all girls are), then less oxygen gets to your brain and it doesn't work as well as it could. Easy to fix. Find recipes that include these ingredients and head for the kitchen.

Egg Fried Rice

This one's full of brain boosters (rice is full of vitamin B, which builds up brain cells. It's easy to throw together and tastes great. Make it when you hit one of those blank moments, when your brain can't take any more and you don't want to be eating with your family (they may ask how the studying's going. . . .).

Ingredients:
1 cup cooked rice
½ cup peas (fresh or frozen)
2 eggs
Salt
1 green onion, chopped
4½ teaspoons sunflower or vegetable oil
Directions:
1. Cook the peas, if using frozen.
2. Beat the eggs with a pinch of salt. Add a little of the green onion.
3. Heat the oil in a wok.
4. Reduce heat. Add the eggs and begin to scramble lightly. Add the cooked rice before the eggs set.
5. Increase heat. Work with a fork to break up the mix.
6. Add the peas and the rest of the green onion. Cook for another minute. Season with salt. Note: Put leftovers directly in the fridge — will keep for 2 days only.

VARIATION: At STEP 6, throw in small cooked shrimp and/or finely chopped bits of cooked chicken and chopped cilantro.

Exam Tip SIX — Eat omega-3s

Omega-3s are the ultimate brain boosters. Find them in oily fish, such as salmon, fresh tuna, mackerel, sardines, and anchovies. They get you thinking sharp and fast and chill you out. So cook up some tasty fish as a main meal or snack.

Smoked Salmon Bagel

One of my favorites. An eating classic. Keep it simple or pile it with extras — why not scramble a couple of eggs? Pile the egg on the bagel before adding the salmon, a slice of tomato, and some arugula.

Ingredients:
1 bagel
Low-fat cream cheese
2 slices smoked salmon
Sliced avocado (optional)
Arugula (optional)
Lemon juice
Pepper
Directions:
1. Split the bagel. Spread with cream cheese.
2. Top with the salmon. Layer up with the avocado and arugula if using. Squeeze on the lemon juice. Season with plenty of pepper. Mmmm.

Exam Tip SEVEN — Snack on the right stuff

When you're stressed out, snacks can help. You'll want to be eating small things at odd times. So get stuff that keeps you going and works for you while you're taking time out. Like dips and crudités. A tasty wrap or sandwich. Toasted bread and peanut butter. Sometimes I make up a plate of bits like nuts, dates, sunflower and pumpkin seeds, raisins, chopped fresh fruit and veggies, and orange segments sprinkled with cinnamon.

Guac and Cheddar Rice Cakes

Is it a snack? Is it a chilling brain-boost? It's both.
Ingredients:
1 recipe Guacamole (page 66)
2 or 3 rice cakes
½ cup grated Cheddar cheese

Directions:
Spread the guacamole on the rice cakes, then top with cheese.

Banana, Cheese, and Honey on an English Muffin

This one works. It's sweet and delicious.
Ingredients:
1 English muffin
Honey
Ricotta or cottage cheese
1 banana, sliced
Directions:
1. Slice the muffin across. Toast.
2. Drizzle on some honey. Top with a dollop of cheese and some banana slices.

VARIATION:
CINNAMON AND BANANA ON A MUFFIN:
At STEP 2, mix some butter, honey, and ground cinnamon together. Spread on muffin and top with banana slices.

Exam Tip EIGHT — Take time out to exercise

Move. Exercise is the best stress buster on the planet. And anything goes. Do some pull-ups. Go for a run around the block. Get out  the punching bag. Work out to some music in your room. Even getting up to have a stretch helps. Walking around clears the brain and makes you feel better. If you're stuck at your desk, lift your shoulders up to your ears, then drop them down three times — breathe out as you do it.

Learn to breathe deeply

Check this out. It works. My mom teaches this exercise to actors and TV presenters who get really nervous, and to people who are feeling really stressed about stuff. Try it while you're studying — it helps you think better. Have it as your emergency strategy to get you through oral exams and to get you going if you panic. What it does is send lots of oxygen to your brain to bring your adrenaline levels down. And it keeps your mind from going blank — not useful when you're staring at that exam paper.

Here's how to do it: Stand in front of a big mirror. Put your hands on your hips. Now move them up to find the bottom of your rib cage. Put slight pressure on the ribs. Now take a deep, silent breath in through your nose. As you do it, make the ribs push out against your hands so the rib cage is expanding sideways — not pulling up. When the ribs have expanded as much as they can, let them come back slowly into position again, while breathing out steadily through your mouth to a count of 15 in your head. You may get a bit of a head rush, so stop if you need to. Repeat three or four times. You should feel really calm and chilled out when you're done. . . .

When you've got the method, do it without your hands or the mirror. Do it when you're in exams or waiting for your turn to present.

Exam Tip NINE — Sleep

Get tons of sleep — it's the ultimate stress release. But hard to come by if you're uptight or if the exam's the next day. So if counting sheep doesn't work, try breathing. When you're lying in bed, take deep breaths down to the bottom of your stomach. Imagine the air's filling it like a balloon. Then let the air out slowly. Repeat a few times. This should clear your mind and calm you. Caffeine could also be the reason you're not able to sleep. Eat to chill out in the evening — stuff like pasta's great. Try spaghetti alla carbonara (page 55). Make yourself a milky drink, like hot chocolate, before bed.

Pre–Exam Night Hot Chocolate

Treat yourself — this hot chocolate works and has barely any caffeine. Froth the top. Delicious.

Ingredients:
Large mug of milk or milk and water
2 ounces dark chocolate
Directions:
1. Put the milk or milk and water into a saucepan on gentle heat.
2. Add broken-up bits of the chocolate.
3. Stir for 3 to 4 minutes, or until the chocolate melts. Use the time to relax.
4. Froth it up with a hand blender or whisk. Pour into mug.
5. Drink. Go to bed. Sleep.

Exam Tip TEN

Eat tactically on exam days

Give yourself all the help you can. Don't try eating or drinking anything new. Don't OD on coffee. Take water into the exams.

FOR MORNING EXAMS:
Have breakfast — peanut butter on toast, egg and toast, fruit, yogurt, or a banana-based smoothie if you can't face anything solid.

FOR AFTERNOON EXAMS:
Nothing too heavy — you'll get sleepy. Eat a light soup with a bit of bread and fruit. Or a wrap or sandwich with a lean meat or light veggie filling.

FOR ORAL EXAMS:
Eat really light food. No coffee or soda with caffeine — it dries the throat and makes you more nervous. No dairy — it clogs up your throat. Sip water before you go in. Sit and do some light breathing exercises.

Essential Extras

Sort out some basic techniques and brilliant eats. These extras make all the difference. Make your own breads, dressings, stocks, and other essentials. Get hooked on real flavors—do it.

Salads need dressing

Even a bit of sad lettuce gets the star treatment with one of these dressings. Try them all out. See what you like. The trick is to match your salad flavors and textures with the type of dressing.

A Great Honey and Mustard Dressing

Feel free to add other extras to basic dressings. You could use cider vinegar here. Or a bit of walnut oil (really good for you, by the way). This one has a lovely sweet-sharp flavor.

Ingredients:
2 teaspoons whole-grain mustard
1 teaspoon honey
1 garlic clove, crushed
2 tablespoons lemon juice or white wine vinegar
Salt and pepper
6 tablespoons olive oil
Directions:
1. Tip all the ingredients but the oil into a jar. Close and shake.
2. Add olive oil. Shake again.

Everyday French Dressing

This makes a great basic dressing. Sometimes we just whisk everything together in a bowl (vinegar and mustard first, oil last). Other times we put it in a jar and shake it.

Ingredients:
2 tablespoons wine vinegar (red, white, or sherry type)
1 teaspoon English or Dijon mustard
1 teaspoon sugar
Salt and pepper
1 clove garlic, crushed (optional)
6 tablespoons olive oil
½ shallot, chopped (optional)
Handful of chopped parsley (optional)
Directions:
1. Stick the vinegar, mustard, sugar, salt, pepper, and garlic (if using) in a jar.
2. Slap on the lid. Shake till it's thick and comes together.
3. Add oil. Shake again. Add shallot and parsley, if using.

On a diet?

Blitz low-fat plain yogurt, herbs, garlic, and seasoning.

Italian Hands-on Dressing

Smash this one together. Using your hands, mix with with lettuce so it's well coated. Good, sharp, and tasty.

Ingredients:
1 garlic clove, minced
Pinch of salt
1 teaspoon balsamic vinegar
5 teaspoons red wine or sherry vinegar
Pinch of sugar
2 tablespoons olive oil
Directions:
1. Smash the garlic to a paste with the side of a knife on a board or in a mortar with a pestle.
2. Put in a bowl or leave in the mortar and add the salt, vinegars, and sugar.
3. Drizzle oil and the vinegar-garlic mix over your salad.

Home Express Dressing

Take your olive oil and wine vinegar to the table. Drizzle oil on first. Then a bit of vinegar.

Oriental-Style Dressing

This one's got a bit of a fizz. Use it all over the place, not just with oriental-style stuff.

Ingredients:

⅓ cup sunflower oil
1 teaspoon sesame oil
4½ teaspoons wine vinegar
1 tablespoon soy sauce
1 small shallot, chopped
1-inch piece of fresh ginger, grated, or a pinch of ground ginger

Directions:

Whisk the lot together.

Basic White Sauce

Essential in the best dishes — like cauli cheese and lasagna. Get it smooth and creamy. Once you know how, it's no big deal.

Ingredients:

4 tablespoons butter
½ cup flour
2 cups milk
Salt and pepper

Directions:

1. Make a roux (fancy name for a mixture of butter and flour): Melt the butter gently in a saucepan. Add the flour gradually. Whisk quickly with a wooden spoon. Cook for 2 minutes on low heat, stirring so the mixture doesn't burn.
2. Take your roux off the heat. Add the milk slowly, whisking continuously, to prevent lumps from forming.
3. Return pan to stovetop.

Increase heat. Bring to a boil and cook for 2 minutes, till sauce thickens, whisking as you go. The sauce is now ready to adapt for your recipe.

VARIATION:

BÉCHAMEL SAUCE: Before STEP 1, heat milk with 1 bay leaf, 6 black peppercorns, 1 peeled, sliced onion, and herbs of your choice. Bring to a boil, then remove from heat and leave covered for 10 minutes. Strain through a fine sieve. Use as the milk in your white sauce.

TOP TIP

Cover the surface of a white sauce with waxed paper or melt a little butter over it to keep it from developing a skin if it's hanging around. Mix the butter in before using.

Pesto

This great sauce multi-tasks: stir it into pasta or rice, use it in sandwiches . . . great with grilled veggies. Loves chicken. You'll need tons of basil. Grow your own outside or in a pot on the kitchen windowsill.

Ingredients:

¼ pound fresh basil
⅔ cup olive oil
2 tablespoons pine nuts
2 large garlic cloves
¼ cup grated Parmesan cheese

Directions:

1. Blitz all the ingredients except cheese in a food processor.
2. Tip into a bowl. Mix in the Parmesan. Cover. Chill.

VARIATION:

Use cilantro or arugula instead of basil.

White Loaf

Hmmm — which is better? The crunchy crust or the soft white bread? I can't decide. . . . Your supermarket bakery should have fresh yeast — just ask.

Makes one 2-pound loaf or two 1-pound loaves
Ingredients:
1 ounce fresh yeast
1 teaspoon sugar
1½ cups warm water
6 cups white flour
2 teaspoons salt
1 tablespoon butter
Directions:
1. Cream fresh yeast with sugar in a small bowl. Add 1 tablespoon of the warm water and cover. Leave to froth for 10 minutes.
2. Chuck the flour and salt into a large warm bowl. Rub in the butter.
3. Add the fresh yeast mix and the rest of the warm water. Mix with hands or a wooden spoon till you have a firm dough.
4. Throw the dough onto a lightly floured surface. Knead well for 8 to 10 minutes.
5. Put the dough back in the bowl. Cover and leave in a warm place for 1 to 2 hours, till doubled.
6. Grease bread pans well. Preheat oven to 450°F.
7. Throw dough back onto the floured surface. Knead for 2 minutes. Divide dough for

2 loaves or leave as one. Put in pans. Cover again. Leave to rise in a warm place until it's just above the tops of the pans.
8. Bake 1-pound loaves for about 30 minutes, 2-pound loaf for about 45 minutes. Turn loaf out and tap the bottom to test if it is cooked — it should sound hollow. If it needs more time, remove it from the pan and stick it back upside down on the oven rack. Cool on a rack.
VARIATION: To use active dry yeast, add one (.25 ounce) packet to the flour at STEP 2. Follow the rest of the recipe exactly, ignoring the yeast packet's instructions.

Shortcrust Pastry

Get sorted. Get shortcrust. That's all your pies, tarts, pastry puddings, and quiches done. Work really fast. Use cold ingredients and a light touch for a crisp, light, tasty, home-style pastry.

Makes one 9-inch pie crust or 4 small tart crusts
Ingredients:
1¾ cups flour
Pinch of salt
8 tablespoons cold butter
2 to 3 tablespoons very cold water
Directions:
1. Sift the flour and salt into a large bowl. Cut butter small. Add to flour.
2. Rub butter into flour lightly with cold fingers till it looks like fine breadcrumbs.
3. Add 2 tablespoons cold water. Mix with a fork till the pastry starts to form. Bring dough together quickly with your fingers. Handle very lightly. Add the remaining water if needed. Wrap in plastic wrap

and leave in the fridge for 20 minutes to chill. Bring back to room temperature.

4. Put dough on a lightly floured board. Roll out with a lightly floured rolling pin.

VARIATIONS:

FOR CHEESE PASTRY:
At STEP 1, add
¼ cup each of finely grated Parmesan and Cheddar cheese.

FOR SWEET PASTRY:
At STEP 2, before adding water, stir in
1 tablespoon sugar and the grated rind of 1 lemon.

Chicken Stock

This is the real thing. Recycle a roast chicken and get yourself a great stock. Makes the essential base for soups, stews, risottos, sauces, casseroles, and gravy.

Ingredients:
1 roast chicken carcass
2 onions, peeled and quartered
1 celery stick, cut into chunks
1 carrot, cut into chunks
3 garlic cloves, peeled
1 leek, cut into chunks (optional)
A few fresh herb sprigs, tied with string (optional)
12 cups water
Directions:

1. Chuck chicken carcass with any fat, gravy, and meat into a large saucepan.

2. Add the onions, carrot, celery, garlic, leek, and herbs, if using. Pour in the water to cover. The pan should not be too full.

3. Bring to a boil. Skim off any scum. Simmer on low heat for 2 to 3 hours.

4. Strain stock through a colander over a large bowl. Cool. Cover with plastic wrap. Chill or freeze.

VARIATION:
If you haven't got a roasted bird, use chicken parts.

Vegetable Stock

Get this into your veggie soups and stews. Use any vegetable except spuds, turnips, or beets. Mix and match with the list below.

Ingredients:
2 large onions
1 celery stick
2 leeks
3 carrots
Juice of 1 lemon
2 garlic cloves
2 teaspoons salt
Few black peppercorns
Fresh parsley sprigs
8 cups water
Directions:

1. Wash and roughly chop all the veggies. Chuck them into a large saucepan with the other ingredients.

2. Bring to a boil. Half cover. Simmer for 1 to 2 hours. Strain through a fine sieve.

Sam's Top 20 Tips

1 Get organized. Check the ingredients, timing, and equipment needed. Read the recipe all the way through before you get started.

2 Butter burns fast. Add a bit of oil to the pan, and keep the heat low.

3 Add a bit of salt to onions to keep them from burning and turning bitter.

4 Get to know your oven. Is it too hot or too cold? Adjust temperatures up or down if you find you need to.

6 Use substitutions if you're missing an ingredient or two. Get creative.

7 Nuke the flour briefly before you start making bread. It helps the yeast.

8 Go easy on the salt. A little lifts flavor; a lot kills it. Put it in while cooking, and leave it off the table.

9 Use lots of fresh herbs — they lift and change flavors. Work out what goes with what. Grow your own.

5 Taste the food as you go through a recipe. How else will you know if it's working out?

10 Leave steaks and joints to rest in a warm place after cooking. This maxes the tenderness and flavor.

11 Take risks. Mix weird tastes. Break the rules. Sometimes the best stuff happens when you experiment.

12 Cooking a whole meal? Work it out so everything's ready at the same time. Grab yourself a really loud kitchen timer, and use it!

13 **Whipping egg whites?** These won't whisk up successfully if there's or any stray egg yolk or grease on your hands or utensils.

14 **Cook more than you need.** Eat it the next day or freeze it

15 **Don't get stressed** if things don't go right — just figure out what went wrong and try again.

16 **Choose your oils well.** Olive is best. Sunflower is good. Use peanut oil for curry and sunflower plus sesame oil for stir-fry.

17 **Put your food in the oven** once it's reached the right temperature, not before.

18 **Don't expect home-made food to look and taste like the stuff you buy in the store.** It'll taste way better, be much cheaper, and be different each time you make it, which keeps it interesting.

19 **Cooking for vegetarians/ vegans/dairy allergies?** Use soy as a dairy substitute. Check the labels on cheese. Search out other substitutes.

20 **Be an artist on a plate.** Making food look really great is all part of it.

For our family and Purdey

Sam would like to thank: Tom Yule (Yuley), Joe Coulter, Nick Howard, Gareth Dowse (Dowsey), Matthew Ford (Fordy), Jess Taylor, Hattie Coulter, Olivia Towers, Hannah Wilson, Hannah Jackson, Margarete Ousley, Riona Naidu, and Daniel Hersi. Thanks also to Laura Morris for believing in this book, and to Denise Johnstone-Burt, Louise Jackson, and Barry Timms at Walker Books.

Photographs by Trish Gant, with additional photography by Lorne Campbell

First U.S. edition 2006. Library of Congress Cataloging-in-Publication Data is available. Library of Congress Catalog Card Number pending. ISBN 0-7636-2988-X. 10 9 8 7 6 5 4 3 2 1
Printed in China. This book was typeset in Vag Rounded.
Candlewick Press, 2067 Massachusetts Avenue, Cambridge, Massachusetts 02140. visit us at www.candlewick.com.